The Good News of Church Politics

The Good News of Church Politics

ROSS KANE

WILLIAM B. EERDMANS PUBLISHING COMPANY
GRAND RAPIDS, MICHIGAN

Wm. B. Eerdmans Publishing Co.
4035 Park East Court SE, Grand Rapids, Michigan 49546
www.eerdmans.com

Printed in the United States of America

30 29 28 27 26 25 24   1 2 3 4 5 6 7

ISBN 978-0-8028-8383-4

Library of Congress Cataloging-in-Publication Data

A catalog record for this book is available from the Library of Congress.

Scripture quotations, unless otherwise indicated, are from the New Revised Standard Version Updated Edition (NRSVue).

For Liz

"In Jesus Christ our Lord you have . . . made us citizens of your kingdom."

—BAPTISMAL SERVICE, *THE BOOK OF COMMON PRAYER*

Contents

Preface

It's easy to find books about Christianity and politics, and it's relatively easy to find books about organizing a congregation or parish. Few speak about the congregation as a center of Christian politics or offer a guide for ordinary church politics, as this book does. It isn't a guidebook in the sense that it gives solutions to any scenario we might encounter; rather, it provides a theological guide to orient how we approach such scenarios. What do politics have to do with discipleship? How can a church organize its internal politics to become a more loving community? When Jesus tells us to love our neighbors, what sorts of public engagements accompany that commandment? In short, the book offers a political theology for congregational ministry. "Political theology" can sound like an imposing term, but in this case it refers simply to an account of politics in light of God. This book gives an account of local church politics in light of God and God's purposes of love and justice.

The book is grounded in my own experiences of church life, primarily in congregations but elsewhere too. I served as a pastor outside Washington, DC, for some years, which meant that politics was never far from people's minds—nor my own, for that matter. Yet it seemed that our preoccupation with nation-state politics of Washington held back our Christian witness sometimes. In some sectarian circles it's hard work to persuade people that such wider politics matter, but we had the opposite problem in my congregation. National politics was the only politics we seemed to think about. That kept us from seeing how much good work we did in politics through ordinary actions. I saw our congregation help struggling neighbors pay utility bills. We opened a Head Start classroom with a spare room in our church. We were slowly facing the racisms embedded in our city of Alexandria, Virginia. We advocated for housing affordability in a very expensive place. These were political actions, grounded in Jesus telling us to love our neighbors and to seek justice.

Working internationally with the church also shaped this book. Many years ago I worked with churches in South Sudan's peace-making efforts, and it always struck me how easily some pastors in South Sudan translated ordinary Christian practices into wider politics for peace. These pastors saw that politics was all around them, in their villages and churches as well as in their nation-state. They also didn't inherit a strong sense of separation between religion and public life as many of us in the United States did. Such integration enabled these pastors to see clearly that Jesus telling his disciples to love their neighbors is a political commandment. It led them to become feisty peacemakers seeking justice. While I've written the book from the perspective of a pastor in the United States, its themes of interdependence emerged from my experiences of living in East Africa and learning from these pastors.

I say all this by way of background because a book about local politics means that matters from my own life and ministry show up across the book. The city of Alexandria, Virginia, appears the most because that's where I've lived and worked since becoming a pastor. Richmond, Virginia, is the second-most-mentioned city since that's where I grew up. Sometimes the examples in the book might appear highly localized to a reader in another part of the country or the world. But I hope that local experiences provide textured detail that general commentary often lacks.

Plenty of books about Christianity and politics read like treatises, and I've tried to avoid that. It's not because I don't like treatises— I teach ethics and theology, so I happen to like them! It's because I'm trying to emphasize the devotional quality of our church politics. These politics are forms of spirituality, for good and ill alike, so I've tried to write in a way that focuses on our spiritual life.

The premise of this book is that new possibilities open up for churches' political witness when we reimagine what counts as political. Politics is not simply about the struggle for control; it's about how we shape a common, interdependent life. If we reorient politics away from undue attention to statecraft toward ordinary politics around us, our churches can become political bodies that love our neighbors, recognize our interdependence, and proclaim the good news of God's justice. Instead of imagining politics as what happens in the halls of Congress and applying that to a congregational debate about how to organize a community yard sale, organizing the church's yard sale should be a model for how we engage politics in our cities and nations.

Part 1 of the book provides that reframing of politics, making the case that our congregations can serve as centers of Christian political activity. The remaining chapters take up important topics of church life in light of these ordinary politics. Part 2 focuses on the relationship between politics and spirituality. Part 3 provides a guide to church leadership and governance based on this approach to politics, while part 4 focuses on connections between local church politics and the wider politics of cities and nations. The book concludes with a vision of heaven, since Christians are ultimately striving toward the politics of that heavenly city. I hope it all comes together to show that if we carefully tend our church communities, our politics can make us more faithful Christians.

PART 1

Ordinary Politics

1

Neighbor Love as Politics

O n a Tuesday morning in February at eleven o'clock, volunteers gather in a church hall with food, silverware, and bowls. One volunteer warms an enormous pot of soup; others put freshly made sandwiches in to-go bags. Another brews coffee. Around 11:45 people from the surrounding community slowly arrive to eat lunch. Some who come are day laborers making minimum wage. For many of these day laborers, free lunch means that they may have enough money to pay their utility bills that month. Others who come are experiencing homelessness.

Each weekday different churches in this community prepare a free lunch, served in the same church hall. Some volunteers come from local churches while others have no religious affiliation and simply want to help their neighbors. Some volunteers are experiencing homelessness themselves. Anyone who comes can get a sandwich, a side, and hot soup. Some take their lunch with them back to their worksite. Others stay to eat together. Volunteers mingle with those eating lunch, discussing which of the regulars has a new outfit or which construction site is drawing day laborers that week. Every now and then, someone strikes up a song on the piano in the corner of the room. This lunch is a picture of struggle and hope in ordinary circumstances. People who have difficulty finding enough to eat share food, stories, fellowship, and a bit of laughter.

We don't often see this work as church politics. It feels too mundane and too local. Serving soup to strangers and friends doesn't involve statewide policy decisions. It's simply an example of churches and volunteers coordinating themselves to serve people who are hungry. Or so we think.

This book is about how ordinary church activities like feeding the hungry are central to a Christian understanding of politics. I define "politics" as the process of sorting out how a community lives together and makes its decisions.[1] At its best, a church is a community of loving interdependence that models a life based on love of God and neighbor. The congregation is at the heart of Christian political life. Congregations can be communities of love and justice—both internally and in relation to our neighbors. Such churches embody good news in politics. They spread the good news of a God who loves God's creatures and brings justice to the downtrodden. We usually associate spreading good news with evangelism, which is exactly what I'm saying. Good Christian politics is a form of evangelism, a form of proclaiming the God whose very being is love and justice.

The book is also about spiritual wholeness and how politics proves integral to such wholeness rather than opposed to it. We never find spiritual wholeness on our own—we find it with and through other people. We find it in community, and any community involves politics. When we get disappointed about community politics, politics itself is not the problem. The problem is the kind of politics we're practicing.

We often see politics as people struggling for control or trying to dominate, but more fundamentally politics is about our interdependence and how we shape that interdependence. Politics shapes social fabric; while bad politics tears that social fabric, good politics heals it. Congregations can play an indispensable role building and reknitting the social fabric that gives wholeness to our lives. That work happens through internal congregational politics and through works of love and justice in our towns and cities.

Such congregational work requires a vision that breaks through the fragmentation that so often accompanies our talk about religion and politics. Dividing religion and politics between strictly separated realms like church and state leaves us fragmented because it treats them as competitive, even though our lives entail multiple citizenships that often overlap with each other. I'm a citizen of a town or a city, and I'm a citizen of a nation-state. My Christian identity is also a citizenship. Baptismal rites across history speak of baptism initiating citizenship in a political association that Jesus calls the kingdom of God or reign of God. We can view these different citizenships—town, city, nation-state, the kingdom of God, and others —as distinct but not fragmented because the reign of God does not compete with these other citizenships. God's reign does not vie for space in this world as other political realms do. God's agenda isn't about someone's victory over someone else; rather, it's about love and justice breaking into this world and giving hope. In the reign of God we cooperate with the Holy Spirit who works for wholeness and healing amid the divisions and rivalries of earthly politics. Christian spiritual life can thereby encompass ordinary human politics while also transcending them. There remains continuity, not fragmentation, between our various citizenships because we approach them all grounded in the single wellspring that is God's love for this world.

"Politics" clearly means much more than statecraft here, despite our tendency to focus so heavily on that part of it. There are losses when we focus exclusively on politics as statecraft. Politics can feel distant from our ordinary lives, as if voting once or twice a year is our primary means of political participation. Such distance can make us feel gloomy about politics since individuals have limited power to enact change on a state level. State politics can also get us caught up in unhealthy partisanship, pushing us to engage community life based on partisan identities rather than people and issues. Partisans can encourage us to make enemies rather than learning to live together as neighbors.

The idea of seeing politics in our local churches is not completely strange, even if it hasn't usually been our emphasis. A pastor of even the tiniest congregation knows that their job sometimes feels like being the mayor of a small town, as different constituencies pull the pastor in varying directions and as the pastor sets a tone that fits local circumstances. Similarly, anyone who has served on their local church's council or board has probably talked about "church politics" and the difficulties of navigating competing interests in their community. I have no illusions about how difficult and tedious such church politics are. But my tongue is not quite in my cheek when I talk about good news and church politics, because if we attend to these politics as spiritual practice, then we can find good news.

Politics permeates church life, and this is a good thing. Our congregations can practice politics not as combat but as sanctified participation in the mutual shaping of common life. Politics applies to the most ordinary parts of church life, from how it organizes internal meetings to how it shares hospitality with neighbors. What we do as individuals and as congregations affects the whole of our community.

Focusing on our local church politics in light of Christian Scripture and tradition also helps uncover political resources in our faith that we often overlook. Our Scriptures and worship carry plenty of political imagery, but we usually don't recognize it as such or we don't know what to do with it. Similarly, Jesus was a highly political figure in his own day, navigating local politics in his ministry with remarkable acuity. And Jesus was killed as a political prisoner of the Roman Empire—a central fact for any Christian politics. Yet oftentimes our church politics mimics our state politics in unhelpful ways. Christians can and should borrow freely from secular politics when it enhances our tradition, but sometimes we borrow the more divisive and even violent aspects of secular politics, without recognizing the political resources within our own tradition.[2]

Finally, seeing politics in our local churches provides rootedness to our spiritual lives. Given that we are finite human beings, focusing on ordinary, local politics is an appropriate place to start. All of us are limited, and so local political participation gives our spirits a deeper sense of place and a more direct means of action than focusing exclusively on national politics. I also happen to think that focusing locally is a good tactic for achieving more wide-scale political change, but that is not my emphasis here. Building faithful Christian witness in churches shows our local communities the divine power embodied in loving our neighbors. Loving our neighbors changes our interior lives, making us more receptive to God's work in the world and deepening our awareness of loving interdependence with others.

Returning to the volunteers in that church hall, they're acting politically as they engage the wider public life of their community, friend and stranger alike. They're also acting politically as they organize themselves and make decisions about how to serve those who come to lunch—any volunteer service that draws from multiple local churches will have to deal with church politics! They're also engaging wider city politics because many people struggle to eat in this city, and local and national policies affect that struggle. This region does not lack food; rather, certain people lack access to food. Having worked in this lunch program, I also know that many of these volunteers advocate for hunger issues in city hall and beyond. Our work does not stay in the church hall; our work in the church hall takes us to city hall. This pattern is very healthy, as local matters of love and justice in one's neighborhood become instigators for engaging politics more widely in one's city and beyond.

In short, politics involves good news because human beings are made to love, and we can love only in community with other people. Those communities will always be political. God meets us amid our politics, not in spite of them.

2

Loving Interdependence

A congregation's own life can offer a locally rooted politics of loving interdependence based in love of God and neighbor. Scriptures and Christian tradition guide this vision of politics.

The earliest Christian writings, the letters of Paul, put loving interdependence at the center of church community life. In one of his preferred images, Paul pictures the Christian community as a body of many parts, all connected and indispensable to its overall functioning. "For just as the body is one and has many members, and all the members of the body, though many, are one body, so it is with Christ" (1 Cor 12:12). Christians are a part of Christ's very body, one with each other. It is a corporate, public, interconnected identity. In the interdependent body of a church community, each of us has a place and no one should claim priority over another: "If the whole body were an eye, where would the hearing be?" (1 Cor 12:17). Paul's rhetoric appears almost comical in describing this interdependence: "If the foot would say, 'Because I am not a hand, I do not belong to the body,' that would not make it any less a part of the body. And if the ear would say, 'Because I am not an eye, I do not belong to the body,' that would not make it any less a part of the body" (1 Cor 12:15–16). Immediately following this description of interdependence Paul gives the famous hymn to love in 1 Corinthians 13, showing how interdependence connects directly to love.

Later writings of the New Testament expand such imagery, especially the Gospel of John. One of the most politically pregnant moments in that gospel comes in Jesus's upper-room discourse in chapters 13–17. It is Jesus's final moment with his disciples before he dies as a political prisoner of the Roman Empire. Here Jesus upends human hierarchies by washing his disciples' feet, for as teacher and savior he serves them. Jesus does not reject the notion of power; rather, he uses his power to uplift others and show divine love.

Jesus then tells his disciples of their dependence upon one another and upon God. In this moment dripping with political significance, Jesus speaks of love and interdependence in Christian community. After washing his disciples' feet, Jesus gives the disciples a new commandment, to love one another: "Just as I have loved you, you also should love one another. By this everyone will know that you are my disciples, if you have love for one another" (John 13:34–35). Shortly thereafter, Jesus tells the disciples that the Holy Spirit will come. This Spirit will continually show them Jesus and the Father, even after Jesus has physically left them. The Spirit will do this in part through the disciples' own interdependence. Jesus tells the disciples, "You will know that I am in my Father, and you in me, and I in you" (John 14:20). Jesus speaks of a loving interdependence that emerges out of human dependence upon God. Like branches, reliant on one another and unable to exist without connection to the vine, our community life is enabled by Jesus's love for us and realized in our love for one another.

The mutuality entailed in this love is not oversentimental but sacrificial. To recognize that our lives are intertwined is to recognize that our needs and others' needs are connected. Sacrificial love of Jesus's sort, modeled through washing his disciples' feet and giving himself to death, becomes the model of human love. It entails a community of mutual sacrifice, in which all parties participate in sacrificial acts. It's not that some sacrifice while others manipulate that sacrifice for their own exclusive benefit—a common problem in Christian communities. As Saint Anthony said some centuries after John's Gospel, "our life and our death is with our neighbor."[1] Our ability to see and know God's love—the very source of our life —comes through our relationships with others. Jesus's words to his disciples are not apolitical; they are words that shape a community of loving interdependence.

One church I know discovered this interdependence first by knocking on their neighbors' doors. The congregation was the largest church in a small town, one of those small towns that's getting smaller as more industries have moved overseas or to larger metropolitan areas in recent decades. Its members felt gloomy because the church was shrinking along with the town. They remembered what life was like when the church was larger—more people, more activities, more life it seemed. One day the pastor and a few congregational leaders decided to take a walk around their neighborhood as a spiritual practice for their church. They wanted to talk with neighbors, hear about how their neighbors saw them, and learn how their neighbors struggled. They started meeting together with other churches in town about what they could do together. A few months later, the church's sense of identity began to shift. Instead of being preoccupied with questions such as, "How large is our church?" or "How many programs do we run?" they started asking how they connect with their neighborhood. They asked, "How are we participating in works of love in our neighborhood?" or "How can we serve our neighbors together with another church across town?" The church had a new sense of purpose. They helped another church rehabilitate an after-school ministry that mentored kids in poverty; they opened their church to neighborhood events. Having been the largest church in town allowed them to be very inward, since for years people just came to them. When that stopped happening, it pushed them to realize how interconnected they were—and always had been—with their neighbors. They were excited to be a church again, feeling that their common life was not just a social gathering but a fellowship whose abundant life overflowed into their community. Their life and their death was with their neighbors.

Saint Augustine takes Jesus's words about interdependence and applies them to both human psychology and politics. Augustine sees love as the defining quality of human beings: we are beings who love. For Augustine, as one theologian puts it, "we are what we love." Humans are "bundles of loves," another says.[2] While many remember Augustine as a gloomy and introspective saint who popularized the term "original sin," we cannot understand Augustine if we do not see the centrality of love to his understanding of humanity. There will be more to say about sin later, but for Augustine even sin is bound up with love. Sin and wrongdoing are misguided and misdirected expressions of love.

All politics for Augustine thus centers on love. Political entities are groups of people gathered on the basis of what they love. This is the case for any human community, from a family to a church to an online chat room to the United Nations. We need not see politics and love as oppositional. The universal church is then a community gathered on the basis of love of God and neighbor, which finds its most local expression in a congregation. That church becomes a subunit of a worldwide, universal fellowship across time, dedicated to love of God and neighbor. Christians practice loving interdependence with one another most frequently in our congregations, which—when done well—enables loving interdependence throughout the rest of our week and the rest of our lives.

In taking these themes from ancient Christianity and applying them today, I focus especially on the theme of interdependence. Putting love at the center of Christian politics is nothing new, but in the contemporary moment stressing interdependence emphasizes the communal character of love and politics. Western politics often highlights individual rights, after all, since individual rights are vitally important to a modern state concerned with justice. This emphasis, important as it is, has a shadow side when it deprioritizes human interconnectedness and gets applied unequally. Isolating the human self imagines the human being primarily as an autonomous rational being rather than a being defined first by its loves. Protecting individual rights is vital to any functioning and just approach to politics, but such protections need not be oppositional to recognizing human interdependence. Our individual lives are constituted through one another, such that our cities and towns are as primary to human life as hives are to bees.

Varying regions of the church have different ways of talking about interdependence, and we can learn from one another. One of the most powerful images of interdependence comes from the notion of *ubuntu* in southern Africa, which means, "I am because you are." My own sense of self is shaped in relation to others around me. They have shaped me and I them. We learn the most basic human capacities like speaking, loving, and reasoning through our relationships with others, not on our own. While I am a person distinguished from these others, these others are also part of me because I know myself only in relation to them. Desmond Tutu writes, "We are made to live in a delicate network of interdependence with one another, with God and with the rest of God's creation. . . . A solitary human being is a contradiction in terms. A totally self-sufficient human being is ultimately subhuman. We are made for complementarity. I have gifts that you do not; and you have gifts that I do not."[3] Many Christians in South Africa then use *ubuntu* as a way of reading Jesus's words in John noted above. Not only are we connected one with another, but we are also caught up in the life of God, who creates, redeems, and sustains us. In Christ we share *ubuntu* because we are all branches in Jesus's vine.

Our churches can become places where we find ourselves caught up in the love God has for us, for our fellow churchgoers, for our neighbors, and for the world. Our Scripture and worship imagine politics in this ordinary fashion, in ways that might surprise us.

3

Public Life in Scripture and Worship

When Christians read our Scriptures and gather for worship, we use all sorts of political language. There are phrases in the Bible that seem innocuous to us today but in earlier historical contexts implied something quite political. Since we've grown used to these phrases, today Christians don't always recognize just how political such language is. Christian tradition embeds politics throughout its life.

In my own ministry, when my church hosts an adult-education event related to politics, one of two reactions nearly always follows. Some people express excitement. They feel glad to have an opportunity to discuss how their faith informs political matters. Others respond with disdain. For them, we've broken a cardinal rule of American politics by blurring the separation between church and state. An irony here is that such separation was intended to prevent the state from establishing a religion, not to prevent religion from having any influence in a state. Retaining institutional separation between church and state is healthy, but that does not imply separating out our spiritual lives from our broader social and political lives. When politics entails more than simply statecraft, we can loosen up our attitudes about how churches relate to public life. Even a word as common as "church" has political origins. The Greek word for "church" in the New Testament, *ekklēsia*, referred to a town's assembly of citizens that made decisions for the community. Christians retooled the word for our own purposes. Our Scriptures and worship can help sort through some of our conflicted responses to church and politics.

In our Scriptures, political imagery shows up all the time. Vital theological categories like salvation, faithfulness, covenant, judgment, and instruction (or *torah*) were highly political words in the Old

Testament. The Hebrew word for "salvation" carried a sense of military victory: in the exodus God's salvation came to Israel as they were delivered from slavery. Faithfulness, *hesed*, was associated with faithfulness to God's covenant. Nations would make covenants with one another in the ancient world, and so the notion of God covenanting with Israel and Israel being faithful to that covenant drew on ancient diplomacy. *Torah* became a way of organizing the lives of Israelites around attention to God. It shaped laws, which are political things. They're means of organizing people and sorting out how a community lives together. Following laws shapes someone into a member of something larger than themselves. Following just laws recognizes human interdependence and, in the case of law based in *torah*, human dependence upon God and the value of human beings in the eyes of God.

New Testament writers use many of these same terms, adapting them to their circumstances. Faithfulness to the new covenant in Christ entails loving God and loving neighbor with actions that build a new community committed to neighbor love, taking root right where we are. Salvation takes on a different quality from military victory, but that does not mean it loses all political connotations. When Jesus rides into Jerusalem on a donkey during his triumphal entry, crowds shout "hosanna" or "save us." When we say that on Palm Sunday, many of us think in terms of Jesus saving our souls, but to many Judeans and to the Romans occupying Jerusalem this salvation was political—they heard "save us from Rome." These calls for salvation from Rome led directly to Jesus's death as a political prisoner. In more mundane events in the New Testament, when people receive salvation they follow suit with actions that reshape the community around them. A tax collector stops his grift; soldiers no longer extort money; the wealthy share their goods (Luke 19:8; Luke 3:14; Acts 2:44–45). In these examples, salvation entails moving a political community away from injustice and closer to loving interdependence.

Jesus speaks in political terms when talking about the "kingdom of God" or the "reign of God." The notion of a kingdom might seem old-fashioned to us today, but for much of Christian history a "kingdom" was something quite clear: a political realm with a king. Jesus speaks repeatedly about what his kingdom looks like—it's a place where the last are first, where vulnerable people are included and cared for, where the poor enter before the rich. Christians have called the kingdom of God all sorts of things—"kingdom," "reign," "commonwealth," "beloved community"—all political terms.

In Luke, Jesus sums up the character of this new community, in the same upper room where Jesus washed his disciples' feet before his execution by the Romans: "The kings of the gentiles lord it over them, and those in authority over them are called benefactors. But not so with you; rather, the greatest among you must become like the youngest and the leader like one who serves" (Luke 22:25–26). The reign of God is a politics where human calculations of status and prestige are always being upended in favor of service and mutual giving.

These themes continue in the epistles, where writers like Paul commend a Christian community of radical equality. When hierarchies begin to form between Jews and Gentiles in these churches, or between those who eat meat sacrificed to idols and those who don't, Paul quickly criticizes such posturing for position. Similarly in James, the author speaks harshly to a community that lifts up its rich at the expense of its poor.

Political dimensions appear across our worship as well. Let's start with the sacraments' political shape. The sacrament of communion forms a society of people who are parts of Christ's own body. "Body" carries multivalent images here. The body of Christ is Christ's presence in the bread and wine, being broken and given for the world. It is also the corporate body of believers as we gather at the eucharistic table. A corporate body takes shape from the act of receiving the body of Christ in bread and wine. We are then sent out to show the world its own interdependence rooted in divine love. The real presence of Christ in the sacrament shapes a society of people who see ourselves as part of God's reign. In receiving the body of Christ in communion, the church enacts the interdependent unity that God intends for our towns and cities and for the world.

The sacrament of baptism also carries political associations. Many baptismal rites speak of Christians becoming citizens of God's kingdom, as noted earlier. Baptism establishes a covenant between a person and God and also between that person and a wider community. In the flow of the baptismal rite, one begins the ritual of baptism as an individual and ends as part of a community. The sacrament of baptism joins us to a corporate body. That's why private baptisms have fallen out of favor for many churches: they obscure the social and political imagery of joining Jesus's movement. In baptism we become part of a mystical fellowship called the body of Christ. Christ's body is a body politic.

Finally, political imagery infuses our hymns. Consider two ancient hymns in Christian tradition, the Gloria and the Te Deum. Both use extensive political language and endure across denominations today. The first line of the Gloria says, "Glory to God in the highest, and peace to God's people on earth."[1] The hymn pictures God uplifted, as on a throne for a king. It then names us as God's "people," a human political community. God has called us to be a society of sorts, spanning time and geography. Then the hymn more explicitly calls God "heavenly King, almighty God," picturing God as one who wields authority on the earth as a just ruler. It asks Jesus to give mercy, as a judge would. It pictures Jesus "seated at the right hand of the Father," that is, with great power next to God the Father as king. In the Gloria, God is king and we are God's people, a society set apart to tell the world of God's goodness and love. In our worship, Christians acknowledge ourselves to be a people, a community, a public thing. We acknowledge the God of love as our king, as our political authority.

The Te Deum has even stronger political imagery.[2] It addresses God as one would address a king in the ancient world with praise and acclaim. Many appear before this king giving honor, as in a political parade. First come the heavenly beings: "To you all angels, all the powers of heaven, Cherubim and Seraphim, sing in endless praise." Then faithful humans pass before God: "The noble fellowship of prophets praise you. The white-robed army of martyrs praise you.

Throughout the world the holy church acclaims you." We still have these sorts of events today in national politics, as when various government officials and constituencies parade before a newly elected president after an inauguration. Jesus Christ, again seated at God's right hand, is uplifted as "the king of glory." The kingdom of heaven is a political body joined together at Christ's throne. Both hymns contain phrases and images, most of which come from Christian Scriptures, that appear time and again in worship across the centuries. However one interprets these hymns, they are infused with unavoidably political imagery, showing how deep the language of politics goes in our worship.

Sometimes people spiritualize such Scriptures, worship, and hymnody, removing any concrete political associations. Israel was a nation in the ancient world, we sometimes hear, but in the New Testament Jesus established a spiritual kingdom rather than an earthly one. This interpretation moves too quickly, however. Terms like "salvation" and "faithfulness" have spiritual associations now, but that does not mean that they lose all concrete associations. The kingdom of God is not a geographic entity like a nation-state, to be sure, for its spiritual quality transcends geography, nation, and history. It's still a political body, however, one that involves material realities like human bodies and negotiations between people. Likewise in worship, it is too simplistic to say that political imagery is only symbolic. Since God is invisible the imagery carries spiritual qualities, but since humans are embodied our worship also forms a visible, material, and public community.

We find political language across Christian Scriptures and worship. Such language shows us the pervasiveness of politics in human life. The Scriptures invite us to see that good politics draws us into mutual life with others and into the very life of God. Good politics proclaims the good news of God's love that lies at the heart of creation.

4

Good News in Politics

We often think of politics as a gloomy exercise. We imagine politicians who seek their own power above all else, something like the television show *House of Cards* where calculating manipulation overrides moral principles. During times of gridlock, we see politics as dysfunctional and exasperating. Our negative associations with politics also arise from misconceptions about power, assuming power is inherently bad. Yet we all have power, however large or small, and can use that power to make our church and our world more loving and more just. Politics does not have to be gloomy, for we human beings are the ones shaping it, and we can shape a different kind of politics. The base of our common life is good, after all. We see this in the ordinary ways that humans care for each other and in the everyday parts of our social and economic lives that function with relative ease. When Christians see politics as acts of re-neighboring—work that heals fragmentation through loving neighbors—we participate in good and life-giving politics.

Much political theory—secular and Christian alike—claims that governments and politics exist primarily to restrain human wrongdoing. Governments' primary function is to prevent us from harming each other. As James Madison famously said, "If men were angels, no government would be necessary."[1] If only we could behave ourselves and treat each other kindly, it seems, there would be no need for the activities of governance, perhaps not even politics.

Yet James Madison misreads angels. When Christian Scriptures and tradition talk of angels, they consistently use political language. Angels exist in ordered hierarchies, with seraphim ranking as the highest, followed by cherubim, and so forth. Archangels like Michael and Gabriel bear significant political powers within such authority structures. When Scriptures call angels "heavenly hosts," they're drawing from military imagery. Angels order a common life. Modern Western Christians may not spend as much time reflecting on angels as Christians of other places or other eras, and for some angels may seem quaint. Yet whatever we make of them, they're portrayed with structures of governance that indicate their interdependence.

In Scriptures, then, sinless creatures like angels have politics. Madison is too gloomy. Sin is not the only reason for politics and structures of governance nor even the primary one. God includes politics and governing as part of our created life because we are interdependent creatures. We are, in Saint Augustine's words, "a little piece of [God's] creation" who depend upon God and one another.[2] Politics is part of God's good world.

Politics becomes good news rather than something to fear or avoid. As much as Christian Scriptures recognize a place for government authority and their laws against wrongdoing (e.g., 1 Pet 2:14), there remains much *more* in Scripture about Christians constituting a political community based in love of God and neighbor. Jesus speaks about the kingdom of God countless times in Scripture, for it is the most significant political image of the New Testament. Paul speaks more about Christians caring for those in need and nurturing the Christian community than he does about governing authorities in Romans 13. Such care among Christian communities clearly involved politics, shown in Paul's monetary appeals for the church in Jerusalem (1 Cor 16:1–4; 2 Cor 8:1–9:15; Gal 2:10; Rom 15:25–31). Christian politics can be about service, about love and justice, and about participating in common life.

Another misconception about politics relates to power: we assume wielding power must involve sin. But power is neutral; it can be used for good or for harm. We exert power in acts both large and small. Feeding the hungry or organizing an event about housing affordability in your neighborhood—these simple deeds are acts of power. We get cynical about power in politics because we see how people exploit it. Yet we all have power, for power is simply the ability to act, to produce some effect. Political power does not reside only in the hands of government officials, as any social movement knows. When we think about power in politics, it's tempting to focus on people who seem to have more power than we do, forgetting the power that we ourselves possess.

The reign of God works through the smallest acts of power, which ripple outward and empower more people to act. In my own city, for example, a few pastors and social workers met one day to discuss how we could better organize food distribution among city agencies and nonprofits. Most churches and nonprofits worked independently from each other, so there were all sorts of duplications and redundancies. We thought of it as a simple planning meeting, but something sparked in that gathering. A few short months later we'd formed an alliance called Hunger Free Alexandria, through which every hunger program in the city connected to this shared network. We started collaborations between city government and nonprofits, as when our city government gave storage and refrigeration space to the city's largest nonprofit fighting hunger. Nonprofits collaborated with one another to avoid duplicating services, thereby opening capacity to meet a wider variety of needs. We formed an advocacy network that addressed hunger needs in city hall and beyond. These were all ordinary acts of power that together formed a new political constituency committed to ending hunger in our city.

Finding good news in our churches and our wider politics requires undoing another common assumption, the assumption that there are differing standards of morality for small communities versus large communities. It's easy to think that love should be the central value for our immediate family life and our church life, but that when it comes to wider politics like city life or national life, love should take a back seat because it's too idealistic. Here we imagine our lives moving outward in concentric circles from family and church life to business life, city life, national politics, and global politics, with the role of love decreasing with each outward circle. Our cynicism about what love can do increases, so our expectations diminish. It is as if the value of love and accompanying virtues like peace, patience, gentleness, and kindness apply only to one realm of life while the wider world is left to cold human calculation.

This idea feels tempting, but notice what we assume when we say things like "the wider world is left to cold human calculation." We're assuming it's inevitable that the world and our politics are this way. We've resigned ourselves. The world feels this way only because human beings are acting in a way to make the world cold and heartless when we could be acting otherwise. Not only have we removed our own agency for love and justice, but we've also given ourselves an excuse for misbehavior by claiming inevitability. We are not just products of our social world; we participate in shaping our social world. The harm we find in the world around us is not inevitable; people are choosing to make it so while others are choosing not to act, refusing to use their power to change something.

When looking for good news in politics, I find it's simplest to start locally. If a political challenge rises to a national level, it's usually an incredibly difficult matter. How does the government relate to the market in large capitalist economies? How do we craft laws that apply to rural farm workers, suburban office workers, and factory workers alike? What role might governments play in health care amid a vast number of jurisdictions and the varieties of human disease? Such national issues prove incredibly complex, which is part of why we get gloomy about what politics can do. Being rooted locally enables us to see more good news in politics. None of this means local politics is friendly and nice—quite the opposite sometimes—but rather that we can see the results of our political work more directly in local and church politics. In local politics we get to know one another as people, not just as a person in one camp or another. Locally it's easier to focus on politics as what we do together, with political debates being a secondary part of that.

Jesus keeps talking about love in politics because we human beings are capable of something more than a world of hatred and violence. We are capable of more than politics based on rivalry and self-defense. When Jesus faced Pontius Pilate before his death, he did not suddenly switch to a different moral calculation now that he faced an official of the Roman Empire. Even when confronting the face of Roman imperial power, Jesus continued promoting self-giving, interdependent love. When Pilate asked what kind of king Jesus is, Jesus said, "My kingdom does not belong to this world. If my kingdom belonged to this world, my followers would be fighting to keep me from being handed over to the Jews" (John 18:36). Saying his political realm "does not belong to this world" is not a pious evasion of earthly politics. Jesus is saying that his reign does not operate by the imperial tactics of Roman rule, and so his followers will not fight. Jesus challenged the very assumptions of Rome's violence, which grounded their rule. The Roman authorities, it would seem, were pleased to get rid of such a preacher.

The good news of church politics is the reign of God that Jesus started—an interdependent human community based in love, a human community that rejects violence in its internal politics, a human community spurred by the Holy Spirit to share the goodness of God's mercy and love. Like Jesus, we too should be willing to die for these things. Christians say that Jesus died so that we might have life, and this is true in politics too. Jesus's own death shows us a way of self-sacrificial love, one that joins us to God and our neighbors. Jesus's way turns politics into an instrument of healing and repair—into good news.

Questions for Reflection and Discussion for Part 1
- Where do you see politics in your congregation?
- How well do you know the neighborhood around your church? Describe your church's interactions with the neighborhood.
- How is your congregation already practicing politics of loving interdependence? How does your congregation's politics inhibit loving interdependence?
- After reading chapter 3, what political imagery do you now see in Scriptures and worship that you hadn't noticed before?

Recommended Reading for Part 1

Augustine. *The City of God.* Book 19, chapter 24. https://www.gutenberg .org/files/45305/45305-h/45305-h.htm#Page_293.

King, Martin Luther, Jr. "A Christmas Sermon on Peace." *Beacon Broadside*, December 24, 2017. https://www.beaconbroadside.com /broadside/2017/12/martin-luther-king-jrs-christmas-sermon -peace-still-prophetic-50-years-later.html.

Williams, Rowan. *Being Disciples: Essentials of the Christian Life.* Grand Rapids: Eerdmans, 2016.

PART 2

The Spirituality of Politics

5

Prayer and Politics

Prayer and politics may seem to have little in common. We often associate prayer with moments of serenity and calm in which we feel an abiding sense of God's presence, and politics with conflict and strife. Yet prayer and politics share many characteristics. Both involve a certain persistence. Both require a commitment to mundane experiences that slowly build transformation. Both require us to let go of our expectations and let the Spirit move unexpectedly. Both push us to recognize our interdependence, in part through listening. It enhances our political practice to recognize these similarities. It also nourishes our spiritual lives. Tending our spiritual lives through politics is the focus of these next few chapters.

We have illusions about prayer and politics alike. We imagine them as dramatic activities while ignoring their ordinary qualities. Portraits of mystical experiences portraying prayer in radiant fashion encourage this kind of thinking. Bernini's sculpture *Saint Teresa in Ecstasy* is a famous example, but not unusual. It shows Teresa of Avila in a moment of prayer with her head turned slightly aside, her body leaning backward. Her robes flow sensually in a moment of union with the divine. In politics we are similarly drawn toward the dramatic. We organize our religious political life around grand rituals like Easter and our secular political life around rituals like an inauguration.

Yet both prayer and politics require persistence, listening, and a commitment to mundane experience. Most of the time prayer is quite ordinary. Contemplative prayer, for example, requires the same act of being still before God day after day. Sometimes the stillness is comforting. Other times it isn't, because I find a part of my inner soul that I'd rather not see. Some days in prayer I feel myself drawn into the very heart of God; other days I barely let go of my mental to-do list. The aim of prayer is not mystical experience but rather putting ourselves in a place where God can work in us. Most of the time that work is fairly ordinary, even dull. Yet persistence pays off over time through a transformed life. Even though Bernini based his sculpture on a writing by Teresa about her mystical experience, elsewhere Teresa warns against putting too much into such experiences. Dramatic moments happen, and we can welcome them when they come. These might be experiences of deep assurance and even moments that change our spiritual lives for years to come. Yet we cannot depend on such experiences. We will be disappointed if we pray with the sole aim of having dramatic mystical experiences. Teresa and other mystical theologians even say that these experiences distract us if we aren't careful, for they lead us to seek these experiences rather than God in God's self.

Most political activity proves similarly ordinary. The free-lunch program I described at the start of this book happens every day. Numbers of participants go up and down depending on various factors such as economic downturns or how many day laborers are working nearby. If people volunteer expecting that numbers will diminish and hunger disappear in our city, they'll be disappointed. But volunteers keep working.

When writing on the practice of contemplation, Thomas Merton said this: "Let no one hope to find in contemplation an escape from conflict, from anguish or from doubt. On the contrary, the deep, inexpressible certitude of the contemplative experience awakens a tragic anguish and opens many questions in the depths of the heart like wounds that cannot stop bleeding."[1] Work in politics sometimes leads to these very same feelings—conflict, anguish, doubt. Such anguish from "the depths of the heart" can include new discoveries of our community's social sins, sins that have shaped our souls and their habits. Such anguish may lead us to discover hatred in our hearts that we have hidden from ourselves. Commitment to political work as spiritual practice reveals our social wounds, just as contemplation reveals wounds within our individual selves.

Like the contemplative, in politics we open ourselves to disappointment—deep disappointment. Just as certain harmful habits in our own selves seem persistent, harmful social habits persist despite faithful work to heal them. Prayer sometimes feels like a waste of time, just as ordinary political action feels like a waste of time when it seems nothing changes. Hunger doesn't go away in our city; racism carries on. Faithful contemplatives keep praying, knowing that God will show up despite ourselves. Faithful Christians do likewise in politics, with the same assurance.

One organization that has transformed my life in this regard is the Richmond Hill community. They explicitly combine commitment to prayer and commitment to political action. Living in an interracial Christian community, they follow a monastic pattern of prayer while working for racial justice in the city of Richmond, Virginia. They carefully listen to God's Spirit in prayer, and they carefully listen to what's happening in the city. They have seen many victories for racial justice as well as many defeats in this city that once served as a blueprint for Black exclusion, emulated by other cities across America. Some legislation moved things forward, some backward. Sometimes it seemed as if things were moving nowhere in Richmond's political life. Yet Richmond Hill kept praying, while engaging in rigorous and determined long-term advocacy.

Sometimes surprising, powerful, and dramatic moments come. As the old hymn says, "sometimes the light surprises the Christian" while in song or prayer—or political action. These moments provide hope and inspire us to carry on in our spiritual and political life. In Richmond, its Confederate monuments came down in what seemed like a single moment during 2020. For people like me who grew up in or near this city—a city whose identity had been so caught up in the southern Lost Cause narrative—it was something many of us did not expect to see in our lifetimes. After decades of fighting racism in this city, this was triumphant. It was a moment to celebrate, one that kindled hope.

Even so, our hope cannot rest upon these occasions, just as Teresa says of our prayer life. Such victories are important but can lull us into forgetting the work still to be done. After Confederate monuments came down, Richmond Hill founder Benjamin Campbell celebrated but also pointed to the work ahead. Campbell would put up with four Robert E. Lee monuments for a single "properly funded" majority-Black public high school in Richmond, he said, a city where inequality has been baked into ordinary institutions like schools, social services, and city planning.[2] There were also many who spent a lifetime fighting racism in Richmond who died with these monuments still up. When those monuments were erected in the early twentieth century, Black leaders in Richmond spoke against them and surely felt a deep sting that tempted them to hopelessness. Yet so many kept hope amid despair. John Mitchell, a prominent Black journalist at the time, wrote that Black Richmonders "put up the Lee Monument, and should the time come, [will] be there to take it down."[3] He was right, though he did not live to see that day.

Prayer and politics also both beckon us to active waiting. While we wait for God's Spirit to change us and change our cities, we cannot just sit around. In contemplative prayer we don't sit in silence letting our minds aimlessly wander. We bring intention to prayer that directs our spirits and leads to the Holy Spirit's work of transformation. Similarly with political action, the Old Testament prophets tell us to prepare the way for the Lord (Isaiah 40). As we anticipate God's action, we make way for it. We build the road for God's work to come through. Prayer and political action both require persistence, patience, and a willingness to face seemingly hopeless times.

Finally, prayer and political action both push us to recognize our interdependence. While prayer can seem a solitary activity, a wholesome prayer life grounds itself within acts of communal prayer, especially worship services like Holy Communion. Monastics who lead solitary lives of prayer are still embedded within a religious community of some kind. The life of prayer enables us to grow into the full stature of Christ (Eph 4:13), which entails growing into Christ's body, a communal body shared with others. Prayer requires community just as politics does.

When contemplation and political action come together, we discover spiritual wholeness amid fragmentation and hope amid disappointment. We see how thoroughly our lives are interconnected with God and with one another. We find ourselves part of something much greater than ourselves, which is the work of the Holy Spirit in the world to heal and repair it. Prayer reminds us that political change does not depend entirely on us and so we can also accept disappointments, sensing the ever-unfinished quality of political action. Short-term disappointment and defeat are never the end of the story. In contemplation and politics alike, I've found that major transformations usually only happen after multiple disappointments or defeats. After we've accepted the disappointments and defeats —sometimes long after—we find major shifts taking place. We may even look back and see that amid losses there was headway we could not perceive at the time.

We cannot control the process of seeking justice and repair in our communities, just as we cannot control the process of contemplative transformation. We have to relinquish control and cooperate with the Spirit. Knowledge of the ever-unfinished quality of contemplation and political action provides reassurance that enables us to enter each without fear. We see that just as transformation in ourselves through contemplation often takes years to come to fruition, so too many works of political healing and repair have taken generations and may take yet more. This is no reason for despair; on the contrary, it helps us see ourselves for what we are—one small piece of the Spirit's enormous work of redemption, and an indispensable piece. Such perspective gives us hope in the long term and also immediate expectancy. We are constantly listening for what God's Spirit will do next.[4]

Different as they may seem at first, prayer and politics share a great deal. They require persistence, patience, an attention to mundane experience, and a commitment to communal life. They are some of the most poignant avenues the Spirit uses to transform our lives.

6

Loving Enemies

Unlike the lawyer in Luke 10 who asks "Who is my neighbor?" no one in the Gospels asks Jesus "Who is my enemy?" We know who our enemies are. It can be tempting for many Christians to think that we don't have enemies, especially wealthy or middle-class Christians raised in bourgeois Christianity—I include myself and much of my own Episcopal Church here. We try to get along with people around us, and many of us come from conflict-averse cultures such that we don't picture ourselves with enemies. Or if we do picture enemies, they're large-scale like Americans imagining the Soviet Union as an enemy during the Cold War.

Jesus assumes his listeners have enemies. And he assumes the enemies are nearby, not far away like the Soviet Union. For some of Jesus's listeners the Roman Empire was an enemy, an occupying force imposing its will upon the Israelites. Some considered fellow Israelites who conspired with Rome their enemies, like tax collectors filling a role in the Roman bureaucracy. Other enemies were even closer to home. Jesus himself faced religious authorities who consistently challenged his ministry and eventually conspired with Rome to kill him. In the end Jesus confronts an adversary in his own inner circle, Judas, who turns on him.

Engaging local politics will almost certainly mean we gain enemies. It's strange and surprising what draws ire in local politics, as unpredictable issues bring up awful and uncivil discourse.

One evening, for example, I sat in a school cafeteria with a standing-room-only crowd, there to discuss *the* hot-button political issue in our city of Alexandria at the time. After an introduction by city staff, the public had their opportunity to speak. One early speaker shouted into the microphone. Others spoke with unbridled outrage. Plenty of people spoke with civility, but many spoke with hostility and fury. If one only read the agony of the speakers without knowing the subject matter, one would think it related to one of the greatest moral issues of our time.

The issue at hand, it turned out, was whether to adjust a road configuration. The city was not building a new road; it was deciding how to modify the flow of an existing one. Changing a road configuration proved more controversial in this city than removing a Confederate statue, which the city did only a few months later with no political resistance to speak of. Everyone in this room knew who their enemies were, and their enemies were their neighbors.

Jesus's advice for such bitterness is straightforward: love your enemies. As Christians engage local politics and engage internal church politics, it will often involve the kind of vitriol and bitterness on display in this school cafeteria. And it will come up at surprising times. We should ready our spiritual lives accordingly.

A common emotion in such circumstances is resentment, one to watch carefully in our spiritual lives. Resentment has positive sides that spur us to seek change, but we should also keep in mind its volatility.[1] Resentment can have a corrosive edge that can turn into bitterness. I happened to support a change in this road configuration, as did many in the seminary where I teach. I did not think that we were ushering in the kingdom of God by changing a road, but I did think it would make a safer street for our students, staff, and families. It seemed an ordinary matter of politics with people having understandably different points of view. But it wasn't just the people shouting into that microphone who were bitter. As the arguments dragged on for months, I became bitter too. This example is from a relatively small matter, which shows how it isn't just the big things in politics that eat away at our spirits. Sometimes small matters bring more bitterness than large ones. Bitterness might begin subtly but slowly take up more and more space in our interior lives. In local politics, national politics, or otherwise, bitterness can lead to internal dialogue in which an opponent or enemy takes up an increasing amount of space in our psyche. At times bitterness consumes our interior life, showing its corrosive quality. Bitterness then clings to our spirits such that we say of another, "I have no need of you" (1 Cor 12:21), leading us away from interdependence.

Loving one's enemies is very personal in the Gospels, and this makes practical sense. In my own life, everyday opponents carry a greater hold than a national enemy like Osama bin Laden ever did. When a longtime friend becomes an opponent on a board or within an organization, it feels closer to me than a national political opponent doing something that upsets me. After all, this friend and I share a history of work and friendship on matters relating to our deepest values. The point here is not to intentionally make enemies in order to love them but to recognize—and love—the enemies we already have. There are already-existing conflicts in our spirit and they reveal who our enemies are, like the longtime friend who becomes our opponent. Finally, it's also worth asking ourselves whether others consider us *their* enemy. Does my uninhibited consumption of goods, for example, make me an enemy of someone who doesn't earn a fair wage? Who in my congregation or organization considers me an enemy, and what reasons do they have for thinking that?

When Jesus tells us to love our enemies and pray for them (Luke 6:27–28; Matt 5:44), in practice I find it's helpful to reverse that order. Praying for my enemies leads me toward loving them. Sheer willpower will rarely get me to love, but prayer will. I've often avoided praying for my enemies because frankly I'd rather ignore them altogether. Yet praying for them frees me from their psychological hold in a way that ignoring them never does. There is no psychological shortcut around our enemies; we have to face our resentment and hatred. Their injuries to us have already shaped us, so trying to dodge their memory cannot lead to healing. Our lives and our psyches are already connected to them, and theirs to us.

Praying for enemies doesn't just change our own interior life; we come to join God's work in their lives. Desmond Tutu reminds us that our enemies are not God's enemies. My enemy depends on God for life as much as I do, and my enemy receives love from God just as I do. There are times, admittedly, when this point feels banal.

One part of me will resist another part, which says, "God loves your enemy." In my own life, that usually happens when I haven't faced squarely my own bitterness and resentment. There's some part of me where bitterness still resides. For many Christians it's tempting to suppress that part of ourselves that resists loving our enemy, but the spiritual life involves facing ourselves, not suppressing ourselves. Perhaps that part of ourselves still needs space to lament or grieve the pain that another person has caused us. Lament and grief are vital parts of moving toward loving our enemies, in that they enable us to recognize the pain that needs healing.

It's also true that our human psyches are complex enough that we can *both* love someone and still be working through our bitterness toward them. Love is so expansive in the human psyche that it can coexist with feelings of bitterness. After all, if human emotions are all based in love, as Augustine and so many in Christian tradition teach, then bitterness and resentment are themselves spurred from love even when they take harmful or unhelpful turns in our interior life. Perhaps that bitterness is spurred on by a love for justice, a response to the times we feel that we've been treated unfairly. Perhaps it's spurred on by our desire for human connection, a sense that our relationship with this other person needn't involve mistreatment. In these instances, continually praying for them slowly moves us toward love.

There are plenty of things that loving our enemies *doesn't* mean. Loving enemies doesn't mean liking them, as Martin Luther King Jr. reminds us.[2] We can love someone, recognize they are God's creature, see our interdependence with them, and not necessarily like them. Nor does it mean that past negative experiences shouldn't inform how we subsequently engage with them. Loving our enemies doesn't mean being deferential or being a pushover. If someone has given no indication that their harmful actions have changed, we should still be judicious and careful with them. We can love an enemy while being savvy. Similarly, if an enemy has wielded power in harmful ways, we should be careful. Sometimes we have to keep our head down when it helps a longer-term goal to do so, all while loving this enemy. Jesus told his disciples to be wise as serpents and gentle as doves, which should be read alongside the commandment to love our enemies (Matt 10:16). We should be wise and prudent enough to read our political environment and act accordingly while still seeking to transform that political environment in the direction of loving interdependence.

Engaging in politics, local or otherwise, will bring out emotions that are unexpected and sometimes vitriolic. The way through such difficult interactions is not to return vitriol for vitriol—not only does that harm our spirits, but it usually isn't politically effective. The way through is to love our enemies as Jesus taught us. Praying for our enemies ultimately becomes a spiritual practice central to Christian politics, one that recognizes our human interconnection.

Ultimately, loving our enemies becomes part of loving our own selves. For if I can love my enemy, I can also love the worst parts of myself. If I have hope that God transforms my enemy, I have hope that God transforms the worst parts of me. Loving my enemies is an act of hope—not only for them but also for me. That's how interconnected our lives are to one another: to love an enemy *is* to love yourself.

7

Forgiveness as Political

Forgiving is a political act, and especially so in churches. If politics is the process of sorting out how a community lives together and makes decisions, then forgiveness is an act of re-sorting. Forgiveness rebuilds community. It's an act in which someone decides not to let their animosity be the determining factor in how they engage that community or decides not to hold another's wrongdoing against them. Its political nature does not take away from how deeply personal forgiveness is. It simply recognizes that forgiveness assumes a community and the desire to be in relationship with that community. Even if someone forgives another and keeps their forgiveness private, a wider community remains implicit within the mind and spirit of the one forgiving. Churches can model community forgiveness and bear witness to the forgiveness that God gives human beings. To do so they must also model truth-telling, an unappreciated element of forgiveness. Forgiveness is one of the central ethical acts of Christianity, vital to healthy church politics.

Scriptures and worship prove our guides, showing how forgiveness occurs as a political act. Most centrally, Jesus forgives his own perpetrators on the cross. As a dying political prisoner he states publicly, in the hearing of the many gathered, that his perpetrators are forgiven by God (Luke 23:34). Even in the act of dying Jesus rebuilds community through forgiveness. And it is not just his killers who become forgiven in this act on the cross; we ourselves become forgiven as those whose sins contribute to the ongoing suffering of Christ in the world today. After Jesus's ascension, the next major act of forgiveness is also public, when Stephen the martyr imitates Jesus by forgiving his enemies before his own death.

Our worship enacts forgiveness in similarly public ways. Our prayers of confession are spoken aloud corporately as a community gathered for worship. We publicly ask to be forgiven because we have "not loved our neighbors as ourselves," in the words of the Book of Common Prayer. We confess that we have neglected the politically charged commandment of neighbor love. Forgiveness is also one of the few ethical actions named in the sparsely worded Apostles' Creed spoken in many worship services: "I believe in the forgiveness of sins." After we confess sins to God and each other and receive forgiveness during Holy Communion, our very next act is to offer peace as reconciled people of God who now share a meal at God's table. Such forgiveness leading to table fellowship enacts the kind of community Jesus calls for—confessing, forgiving, and reconciling community. The whole trajectory of communion beckons us to enact in the world what we do in worship.

Despite all this, forgiveness is not something churches talk much about in my experience. Or at least we do not talk much about forgiveness within our congregational life. We talk about forgiveness in smaller community matters like a couple forgiving one another.[1] And in sermons we might talk about someone famous like Nelson Mandela forgiving their enemies. Yet if we do not talk about practices of forgiveness within our own church, people can get the impression that churches think forgiveness is largely about individuals forgiving one another, whether a spouse or a national enemy like Osama bin Laden, and doesn't necessarily involve politics of the medium-sized communities that shape so much of our lives. This omission overlooks ways that a community's interdependence relies on forgiveness.

Even if we do not talk much about forgiveness in church life, there are reasons to be hopeful. If my parishioners were simply terrible at forgiving each other—worse than the general population—there would be more to worry about. But in most churches I know, there's plenty of forgiving going on. We just don't talk much about it or name it. A church board gets into a heated argument during one meeting, and in the next meeting the members decide to put aside their animosity and work together for a shared purpose like renovating a church hall in part to welcome more strangers into their church. Someone becomes disillusioned by her church's tepid response to injustices in the community but keeps showing up in church and advocating for a more comprehensive approach to outreach ministries. A congregational constituency disagrees adamantly with its pastor and leadership but decides not to leave the church because it's a community of people they love. I've seen all these things happen in churches—over and over, in fact—and each of them involves some kind of forgiveness as people decide not to let their animosity toward others define their relationship but instead move forward in hope. It's less that we do not forgive each other and more that we overlook the ordinary acts of forgiveness that sustain a congregation. The good news is that forgiveness is more present than we realize, such that naming the ongoing forgiveness in a congregation becomes one way to recognize the centrality of forgiveness in church politics.

Recognizing existing acts of forgiveness is only the beginning, however, since it takes much more to build and sustain a forgiving congregation. It requires ongoing practices of forgiveness and reconciliation in ordinary church life. Many such practices come up later in this book—refusing to ignore conflicts by shoving them under the rug, carrying out corporate self-examination to ask how a congregation has contributed to sin and brokenness in its neighborhood's life, facing parts of a congregation's history that feel uncomfortable, and so on.

Central to all these acts is the practice of truth-telling in forgiveness. Churches often struggle with truth-telling since they carry a seemingly natural tendency toward stasis and equilibrium that prefers not to dig up what seems uncomfortable. Yet facing difficult histories, recognizing harmful habits of paternalistic leadership, confronting awful abuse—these cannot be avoided in becoming a forgiving and reconciling congregation. Desmond Tutu speaks eloquently about truth-telling's role in forgiveness and reconciliation. The name of the Truth and Reconciliation Commission in South Africa was itself significant to him, down to the word order that put truth before reconciliation. There is no shortcut around truth-telling when moving toward reconciliation, for without knowing and facing the truth we avoid the very sins we must confront. Tutu says, "The past, far from disappearing or lying down and being quiet, has an embarrassing and persistent way of returning and haunting us unless it has in fact been dealt with adequately. Unless we look the beast in the eye we find it has an uncanny habit of returning to hold us hostage."[2] Indeed, some have said that the Truth and Reconciliation Commission he chaired was more of a truth commission than a reconciliation commission because it focused on bringing wrong-doing to light and because reconciliation still has so far to go in South Africa. But Tutu saw that truth-telling was the necessary first step. And his insights about the centrality of truth-telling for forgiveness apply to smaller communities like congregations. A congregation must tell the truth about itself and face its own difficulties and sins to become a community of forgiveness.

This kind of truth-telling should be treated as a spiritual exercise. We are accustomed to recognizing the spirituality of truth-telling in our individual lives, but it applies to our collective lives as well. The truth-telling required for forgiveness within communities is not so different from the truth-telling required for individuals reconciling our own psyches in our spiritual journeys. Just as an individual must face various parts of one's own self that they prefer not to face, so must a community.

Mystical theologians in Christian tradition speak of a continuing cycle moving between purgation, illumination, and union in our spiritual lives, with us moving between these places at various times. These also apply to the spirituality of communities. Purgation entails cleansing and purifying ourselves through purging those things that take us away from God; illumination entails seeing new aspects of God's work in us; and union entails joining with the divine life itself. Often what makes this process hard is that it beckons individuals in the community to do difficult interior work—to go through these same experiences of purgation, illumination, and union—and people can feel threatened by the kind of purgation that truth-telling requires. The work is uncomfortable and demanding. Acts of purgation lead to new illuminations of the divine at work in us, and yet such illumination can shed light into places we had not thought to look before, revealing cracks and darkness we had not noticed. Seeing such darkness may take a community back to purgation.[3] We move between purgation and illumination with knowledge and hope that union does indeed await us—and even meets us in this life, however fleetingly. Congregations move between purgation, illumination, and union as we strive to be forgiving communities.

One congregation I know, for example, had a history of pastors coming through and staying only a few years before leaving. The pattern centered on a core constituency who resisted sharing leadership with the pastor. One new pastor, after a harrowing first six months, stepped back and decided to talk with churchgoers about their resistance to change. He found that years earlier there had been a pastor who badly mismanaged finances and misappropriated large sums of money. During that crisis, these lay leaders took over key parts of finance and administration. While this arrangement stabilized the church at the time, no one led the congregation through a process of grief and lament. These lay leaders felt hurt but also wanted to put the situation behind them, and so they didn't face their feelings of betrayal. The church had not engaged in truth-telling, and so they did not even realize the deep bitterness they still held against their old pastor. Because they had not released that bitterness, they expressed it by resisting change from each new pastor. There was no future without forgiveness for this church, but without truth-telling they didn't even realize that forgiving was their next step toward healing. Their way forward involved communal purgation, illumination, and union.

As our Scriptures and worship suggest, ordinary acts of forgiveness entail more politics than we initially realize. Truth-telling and forgiveness can lead congregations to new places of healing and witness. Through forgiveness, carefully tended church politics can make us witnesses of good news.

8

Tangles of Forgiving

F orgiving is complicated. It's complicated in part because it
involves so much of our own selves. It involves our emotions,
our spirits, and our minds—notably our memory. Memory
is a deep part of identity, and forgiveness asks us to re-sort that
memory using our full selves. Add to this the uncertain questions
surrounding forgiveness. Can we forgive if someone hasn't asked for
it? How much power does a victim have vis-à-vis a perpetrator? Can
we forgive if someone hasn't clearly injured us? Since forgiveness is
so central to faithful church politics, it's important to consider its
difficulties.

Many theologians and philosophers have carefully delineated
processes about the specific steps required for forgiveness or have
strict definitions of what forgiveness is and what it isn't. Yet to me
it seems better not to make the notion of forgiveness or the process of forgiving too rigid. Clearing up misconceptions is one thing;
making forgiveness more difficult than it should be is another. The
occasions for forgiveness are so varied that it seems better to see the
nature of forgiving as capacious and flexible.[1] Forgiving someone
for a snarky remark during a church meeting is utterly different
from someone forgiving a church for its cruelty against them as a
queer person. Beyond describing forgiveness in the vaguest terms,
I don't think there is a singular description or delineated process of
forgiving that covers such wide differences. So here I engage only a
few misconceptions about forgiveness in Christianity and some of
its complications, especially those that relate to congregational life.

One misconception about forgiveness is that it minimizes wrongdoing by not taking that wrongdoing seriously enough.[2] The idea is
that someone putting the past behind them could mean overlooking

the harm committed. Overcoming animosity, however, does not entail overlooking harm. Much of the power of forgiveness is in the fact that someone takes seriously the wrong committed and still somehow overcomes their ill feelings. In many cases forgiving displays a certain wisdom in that the forgiver realizes that forgiveness may be the only path forward for them to live a full life. Sometimes a sin is so great that it cannot be put right, and yet someone has still found a way to face a future in which the past cannot be resolved. Forgiveness recognizes our finitude and inability to change the past and still finds some way to seek wholeness for ourselves and our community amid that past.[3] But that need not, and should not, involve minimizing the past.

Think back to the example in the last chapter of the church whose pastor stole funds. Even though the pastor later had to pay back much of the money, the hurt and the betrayal were deep enough that the congregation still felt the past wasn't entirely put right. Their new pastor, along with Mennonite facilitators, led the church through a process of seeing that their only way forward was to forgive their old pastor and those who enabled him. This forgiveness did not minimize the wrongdoing; if anything, the process of forgiving helped the church recognize the extent of it. Then they could begin to heal. Forgiving doesn't overlook wrongdoing but faces it squarely.

Another misconception treats forgiveness in a shallow or sentimental way, an unhealthy habit that expresses itself in glib expectations that Christians forgive quickly without facing the spiritual and inward difficulties of forgiveness. It's as if forgiveness is like flipping a switch when it's more comparable to lighting a campfire in the rain. Forgiveness is a process—a long, arduous, and sometimes incomplete process. Christians have used forgiveness quite destructively in this regard, insisting on forgiveness by a victim without addressing the wrongdoing of the perpetrator. But this glib approach to forgiveness ignores Jesus's message of justice. Forgiveness can be an act of power by the victim and a means of a victim expressing their own agency. Forgiveness is not something a perpetrator demands but something a victim freely gives.

In a related matter, some say that a victim cannot forgive on their own; forgiving must depend on someone asking for forgiveness. Yet this seems an instance of making forgiveness more difficult than it should be. The biblical justification comes from Luke 17:3–4, when Jesus names repentance and forgiveness as joined activities. Yet the Scriptures are not of one mind on this matter. Matthew's telling of this teaching takes a different approach, with Peter asking Jesus whether he should forgive another as many as seven times, with no mention of someone seeking repentance. Jesus simply says, "Not seven times, but, I tell you, seventy-seven times" (Matt 18:21–22). The perpetrator's contrition is certainly preferable, but the victim should not be constrained by such a requirement. Since forgiveness is a means of reorienting one's spirit away from a perpetrator's hold, the victim should not have to wait for a perpetrator to act in order to free themselves from the trauma inflicted by that perpetrator.[4] Oftentimes the victim has suffered enough and the perpetrator should not have any more power in the situation. To make the victim wait for the perpetrator puts the perpetrator back into a place of power and robs the victim of the spiritual opportunity and freedom that forgiveness brings.

Finally, sometimes Christians claim that forgiveness entails looking at someone as if their sin is not there.[5] This approach minimizes sin, however, and asks strange things of human memory. There are some sins connected to a perpetrator that should be remembered after they're forgiven, whether minor or major. If I say something terse and dismissive to a stranger who visits my church, they have reason to look for another congregation even if they've forgiven me. Or in major cases like sexual abuse, victims have every right to connect a person with their acts of abuse and avoid them accordingly. One can forgive and still respond judiciously to a perpetrator. In many situations, it is hard enough to put aside one's animosity; asking for someone to act as if another's sin did not occur strains the realities of human memory and disregards a victim's safety. Forgiving does not imply people must ignore their own security and wellbeing vis-à-vis their perpetrator. We should ensure that Christian forgiveness prioritizes a victim freeing themselves from past harm. This priority still has space for the perpetrator seeking relief while keeping appropriate focus on the victim.

When discussing forgiveness in church life, one frequent situation is whether we can forgive if a situation did not involve clear or direct wrongdoing. Such a situation would involve animosity or hurt feelings, but it's unclear whether someone wronged another. In the last few instances, forgiveness assumed situations with clear victims and perpetrators. Yet sometimes those roles are not so obvious and especially in ordinary church life.

What do these situations look like? Say a senior colleague in my ministry like a head pastor makes a decision that I completely disagree with, or I make a decision that she completely disagrees with, and we feel animosity toward one another. It's hard to say one of us is a perpetrator and another a victim if we have not directly harmed each other or someone else. In many such instances, it's a matter of one person's human limitation expressing itself in church decisions and another's human limitation seeing that decision as the wrong one. Or say someone in a church feels hurt by another's words or actions even if that person did not directly harm them. Perhaps the action brought up a hurtful experience from a past church community or from their family history. Responses in such situations look and feel like forgiveness, since we decide to let go of our animosity and not hold someone's actions against them. But is forgiveness the paradigm if it's not a clear case of wrongdoing?

I think forgiveness is the right paradigm for such situations, since humans cannot always clearly distinguish between matters of sin and finitude—a matter we take up later on. Sometimes an act done out of the nearsightedness of our human finitude will lead to sin whether we realize it or not at the time. Perhaps my decision in a church meeting seemed innocent enough but later set off a series of events that led to harm. Other times we will have to choose between two wrongs and not realize that's what we're doing. Sometimes our acts will be clumsy and we won't know their consequences. Since it's difficult to know when some acts will lead to harm—and since sometimes we sin without realizing it—it seems we should not constrain the breadth of forgiveness. We can let go of our animosity regardless of whether someone has committed a clear act of wrongdoing. This forgiveness is of a different kind from forgiveness that involves clear and awful wrongdoing, but our spirits can still forgive. Just because it isn't paradigmatic forgiveness does not mean it isn't forgiveness at all.

Christians have often made forgiveness too easy or too difficult, making forgiveness cheap on the one hand or legalistic on the other. We should expect forgiveness to be difficult, but we should not get in its way. For forgiveness recognizes that our humanity is interconnected to such an extent that the animosity we hold against another person ultimately wears away at our own souls too. To forgive another person is to free ourselves from bitterness, anger, and the desire for vengeance. Forgiveness is an act of hope because it imagines a new future in which someone's wrongdoing no longer defines them or us. Churches can be places where we practice forgiveness, even as many as seventy-seven times.

Questions for Reflection and Discussion for Part 2

- When have you seen connections between your spirituality and your public life?
- Who among your enemies is difficult to pray for? Why is it difficult to pray for them?
- What practices of forgiveness are already taking place in your congregation but going unrecognized?
- What kinds of truth-telling should your congregation undertake in its journey toward healing?

Recommended Reading for Part 2

Salzberg, Sharon, and Robert A. F. Thurman. *Love Your Enemies: How to Break the Anger Habit and Be a Whole Lot Happier.* Carlsbad, CA: Hay House, 2014.

Tutu, Desmond, and Mpho Tutu. *The Book of Forgiving: The Fourfold Path for Healing Ourselves and Our World.* Edited by Douglas Carlton Abrams. New York: HarperOne, 2014.

Underhill, Evelyn. *The Spiritual Life.* Harrisburg, PA: Morehouse, 1955.

Zehr, Howard. *The Little Book of Restorative Justice.* New York: Good Books, 2015.

PART 3

Renewing Leadership through Good Politics

9

Habits of Faithful Politics

We now imagine what church leadership and governance look like when our local churches are central to Christian politics, with the congregation as a localized expression of God's in-breaking reign. This approach begins by seeing the most ordinary circumstances as places to practice our politics of love. Ordinary church activities like meetings or outreach campaigns become central to building beloved community and thereby showing God's love to the world. These ordinary activities also help us realize how much everyday actions shape our moral lives beyond politics. Our congregations become places where we shape habits of faithful politics amid ordinary life.

Let's start with something mundane but vitally important: meetings. Meetings profoundly shape our politics and our communal spirituality. Many congregations and organizations in my own Episcopal Church organize meetings around Robert's Rules, a guide based on rules of the US Congress. It's procedural and parliamentary in style, well established and predictable. It can be an efficient way to hold meetings, especially when time is limited for a large gathering. Yet its procedural emphasis also obstructs practices of community building. When a difficult conversation arises, one constituency can press matters forward and thereby suppress conflict and strife. Other times people in one political camp can dominate the conversation—while staying within the rules—and inhibit a discussion that's more representative of the wider group. My church's regional body uses Robert's Rules for large gatherings, and during times of conflict people used them to prevent genuine dialogue across differences such that many people didn't feel heard. People would use Robert's Rules to hijack conversations or avoid facing people they disagreed with. From an intercultural perspective, those who come from congregations and cultures familiar with Robert's Rules have a clear advantage in negotiating given their familiarity with the process. Often the practical result is that conflicts we've avoided carry on through side discussions—our classic church parking lot conversations. People cannot engage interpersonal community building during large gatherings, so smaller political cliques form.

It seems better to use a variety of procedures for church meetings, the choice of which depends on the matter at hand and what the community seeks to achieve. For difficult conversations in which a community must nurture a sense of trust, Robert's Rules is not the best resource. Perhaps after those difficult conversations have already taken place, an organization might return to Robert's Rules when a decision is finalized. For those more difficult conversations one could use resources from, say, the Mennonite Church—a denomination well schooled in addressing conflict—or from a trusted facilitator outside one's group who is able to identify and name a community's dynamics for both good and ill. When deciding on such procedures, the pastor can ask, "What kind of community and what kind of people does this process shape us to become?"

The Anglican Communion's Lambeth Conference of 2008 offers an example of adaptive leadership with church meetings, albeit on a large scale. During the height of disagreement about same-sex relationships in the Anglican Church's sacramental life, the organizers of that conference deliberately moved away from the parliamentary-styled procedure of previous Lambeth Conferences. Organizers from South Africa helped adapt a South African practice of conflict resolution called *indaba* to an ecclesial context. An *indaba* emphasizes interpersonal aspects of negotiation rather than leading with policy matters. It provides space for voicing differing opinions while also including practices of community building. While many expected the Anglican Communion to break apart at the 2008 conference, it did not. Bishops spoke about the depth of relationship building across difference that they experienced. Bishops and other church leaders continued to meet in smaller settings after Lambeth 2008 through groups called "continuing Indaba." The *indaba* process wasn't perfect; for example, bishops less comfortable with the shared language used during *indaba* (usually English) struggled to feel connected. And when adapting to environments outside South Africa, *indaba* should be used in ways respectful of its cultural origins and attentive to the cultural environment in which it's being employed.[1] Nevertheless, Lambeth 2008 showed that matters as seemingly simple as planning the procedure of a meeting have profound effects on politics. It provided a model for practicing loving interdependence during conflict and strife.

By looking more carefully at corporate practices like meetings, we see that in churches we find nearly all the experiences that go into human politics more generally but on a smaller scale. Any institution is a microcosm of the macrocosm of human politics. It's one of the perplexing, fascinating, and joyful parts of church life. The negotiating and organizing of politics, matters of authority and leadership, difficulties with tragedy and sin, disappointment and hope, works of love and justice—it's all here in a church, just like in town or city politics. Human psychology is similar enough across varying circumstances that group dynamics prove remarkably similar whether in a church board meeting, a city council meeting, or the halls of Congress.

As another example of a congregation being a microcosm of human politics, think of a church responding to an issue like the growing need for early childhood education in its community. My congregation faced this issue since our city had wide disparities in access to early childhood education that contributed to wider disparities in economic opportunity. Through conversations over coffee in our emergency assistance programs, we heard over and over how difficult it was for parents to both work and find affordable care for their young children. Our congregation had a long history of working in early childhood education, so that struggle resonated with our church's priorities, and we had internal expertise to respond.

Our response resembled a process that a city government might go through when initiating a new program. An ordinary matter

spurred a community to rethink its priorities. As more people recognized this need, they built constituencies in our church, just as
in city politics. In this case, a single constituency formed that slowly
gained traction across our congregation. In other instances people
might build multiple constituencies, and the differing approaches of
these constituencies shape the wider community's response. Most
of this constituency building happens in ordinary places, such as
over coffee or lunch between acquaintances and friends. In our case,
the congregation soon partnered with a local nonprofit to house a
Head Start classroom for children in our neighborhood. One of the
greatest challenges facing this nonprofit was space because rent
was so expensive in our city. Our church could provide institutional
support as a new partnership formed between our church and this
local nonprofit, which itself partners with both local and federal
governments. When such an initiative takes place in a church, we
usually consider it ordinary church life without necessarily noticing
the politics. When it takes place in city government, we recognize
the politics more clearly.

Given such similarities between church and city politics, many
lessons from ministry apply to the politics we'll experience in towns
and cities. Group dynamics amid conflict and change prove remarkably similar whether in a congregation, a city, or a state. There will
reliably be a significant constituency that resists change, and leaders
should organize and strategize anticipating this resistance. Groups
within a congregation such as its boards go through the same stages
of development as groups on a citywide committee or school board.
First they form themselves, then they set norms. Later a group's
arguments and disagreements start to shape its identity, which can
ultimately help group functioning since such arguments clarify its
sense of purpose.[2] In such environments human elements shape
policy. Interpersonal dynamics play into policy decisions, and leaders' personalities mean that decisions take one shape rather than
another since politics isn't only about ideas and tactics but also about
personalities and quirks. Unexpected matters redirect or derail an
initiative, such that leaders have to remain adaptive and flexible.

This focus on ordinary circumstances requires a reorientation regarding what matters in politics. Some people get involved in local or national politics because it feels exciting and important—we like rubbing shoulders with important people or enjoy the sense that we have sway in public life. This feeling can be motivating, but it can also distract us from healthy politics, especially so in our churches. Politics is not always exciting. Sometimes good politics should be boring. Sitting through a church board meeting and discussing subjects that do not necessarily interest us can be a spiritual discipline that shapes us to recognize our interdependence since other people's interests may not seem important to us but still relate to the well-being of our community. Politics isn't only about rallies and passing big legislation; it entails the everyday work of building and rebuilding communities and constituencies. For churches, the most ordinary events in our common life—not necessarily the dramatic ones—shape us into people of love and justice.

Realizing the importance of mundane matters like meetings and outreach campaigns relates to a larger moral lesson beyond politics as well. We're tempted to think that making moral decisions primarily means getting the big decisions right—what policy gets passed, the career we choose, or how we respond to major crises. These are important, of course, but most of our moral lives are shaped by how we respond to everyday circumstances. Even major moral decisions usually come after an accumulation of much smaller ones. We don't usually get married after spending one remarkable day with someone. We get married after spending many ordinary days doing ordinary things with our beloved. Even a particularly memorable day —one that couples recall again and again—is usually a beginning to a romance solidified later through ordinary life together or is built upon many ordinary days before it.

In sum, caring for church politics feels a bit like how the Confucian tradition talks about building virtue: it's like tending a garden. Not only do we plant and reap—the good stuff—we also till and weed. We cultivate those parts of our church politics that build up love and weed out what's destructive. It's a laborious process, and it sometimes feels like the weeding never ends no matter how loving our churches become. Yet this ordinary work slowly builds up the reign of God. Things like ordinary meetings and outreach campaigns shape the habits of our church and our spiritual lives. Tended well, they deepen our interdependence and shape churches of love and justice.

10

Love as Political Power

Jesus navigated political systems large and small with both love and savviness. His savviness never hindered his love; rather, it increased the potency of his love. Many church leaders, myself included, have yet to fully internalize Jesus's political sophistication in this regard, but doing so helps us see how ordinary events in the Gospels were instances of Jesus dealing with local politics. Jesus's example in turn helps us navigate our local church politics with more attention to love and justice. In the Gospels Jesus offers a master class in nonviolent confrontation when responding to difficult situations.

When reading Jesus's parables and teachings, we can overlook how deftly he handles political opponents like scribes and Pharisees. Jesus clearly knew how to read a room. Think of the times he has a sympathetic crowd around him and uses it as security to challenge his opponents, knowing that the crowd won't let the chief priest and elders hurt him (Mark 12:12; Luke 19:47–48). Sometimes Jesus gives a playful response to challengers, thereby diminishing the force of their questioning without needlessly exacerbating conflict. When authorities challenge Jesus by asking by whose authority he's acting, for example, in return he shrewdly asks them a provocative question about John the Baptist, one he knows they can't answer without harming their own political appeal (Luke 20:1–8). Other times Jesus disarms his critics by undercutting an assumption of their question, thereby diminishing their influence (John 8:6–7; Matt 22:23–33). When situations call for direct confrontation, Jesus sternly challenges his opponents as in his seven woes against the scribes and Pharisees (Luke 11:42–12:7). Jesus always seems aware of the power dynamics around him. Jesus addresses his opponents directly yet nondefensively, even in the most difficult of circumstances.

In these examples from the Gospels, Jesus shows a wide range of tools available to build up loving interdependence amid conflict in church or local politics. Jesus constantly adapts his approach according to circumstances, avoiding violence in favor of loving interdependence. We can adapt Jesus's approaches for our circumstances. If my church leaders are holding on to old ways of doing things and resisting change, as the pastor I can slowly build another constituency within the congregation, a constituency of risk-takers who see differently. Jesus did this kind of thing himself—building a new constituency by working both within and outside given political categories of his day. As Jesus welcomed Nicodemus (John 3), someone allied with Jewish authorities and sympathetic to Jesus, a pastor can identify those who are open to a new approach to leadership and church politics. It should be said that a similar strategy can also work for lay leadership when the pastor is holding on to old ways of doing things and resisting change!

Jesus also provides models for how to respond when someone with authority wields power wrongly. Jesus faces such a scenario before Pilate and offers different responses in different Gospels. Each gospel account provides a strategy for confronting such a grim political situation. In the Gospel of John, Jesus speaks directly to Pilate by telling Pilate how marginal his authority is in comparison to the power of God. Yet in Matthew and Mark, Jesus offers an initial response to Pilate and then responds to further questions with a deafening silence. Matthew says, "He gave him no answer, not even to a single charge, so that the governor was greatly amazed" (Matt 27:14). In some instances one might respond directly to someone with authority over us; in some instances silence itself is a form of communication.

In the trial narratives Jesus also reframes Pilate's assumptions about power. Pilate sees power as force—imperial force at that—but Jesus sees power emanating from God. Pilate imagines authority through human kings and emperors while Jesus imagines authority through nondefensive and interdependent love.

Like Jesus, we can combine love and savviness in our church politics. Say a pastor has to respond to a situation in which a group actively dominates the congregation by disrespecting other members and groups who disagree with them. Tactics vary according to circumstance, but seeing the politics at play enables a prudent response. In the moment when someone speaks disrespectfully in a meeting, the pastor can defuse the situation to address that one action, yet how they respond long-term would vary depending on that moment and the state of the church's other constituencies. If the disrespectful person has a significant number of allies behind him in the room and the pastor does not, then the pastor might not immediately confront this wider conflict after defusing the situation, realizing that she needs to build up her own constituency before a direct confrontation. Or perhaps the pastor has been preparing for a moment like this for some time and has a constituency solidly behind her, in which case she may decide to confront the situation then and there. Perhaps the person best placed to respond is the pastor herself, perhaps a lay leader. When responding to people doing harm, we have not left the realm of loving interdependence. We need not suddenly switch moral gears into Realpolitik but rather recognize that these actions hold back the community's loving interdependence.

Jesus's diverse strategies for engaging politics have led to strategies in Christian politics like Martin Luther King Jr.'s Ten Commandments of Nonviolence. We often think of King's strategies in relation to city or state politics, but we should see them as strategies for church politics too. King implores us to refrain not only from physical violence but also from violence of heart and tongue. He suggests we treat enemies with courtesy, even when they harm us. King also reminds us that the aim is not our own short-term perceived political victory but the longer-term aims of justice. These are his Ten Commandments:

1) Meditate daily on the teachings and life of Jesus.

2) Remember always that the nonviolent movement in Birmingham seeks justice and reconciliation—not victory.

3) Walk and talk in the manner of love, for God is love.

4) Pray daily to be used by God in order that all . . . might be free.

5) Sacrifice personal wishes in order that all . . . might be free.

6) Observe with both friend and foe the ordinary rules of courtesy.

7) Seek to perform regular service for others and for the world.

8) Refrain from the violence of fist, tongue or heart.

9) Strive to be in good spiritual and bodily health.

10) Follow the directions of the movement and of the captain of a demonstration.[1]

These Ten Commandments combine prayer and political action. They show an openness to where God's Spirit is going. Being immersed in prayer amid political action allows us to let go of the need to win or control the process, which gives more room for the Holy Spirit to work. I've seen many forms of political and community organizing that focus almost exclusively on victories, thinking that if they can form the perfect coalition with just the right actors, they will win. This approach falls into politics as a struggle for control rather than politics as interdependence. We find freedom and creativity in our actions when we give up the need to control the process. After decades of prayer and political organizing in Richmond, Virginia, Benjamin Campbell of Richmond Hill said, "I don't need victory. I just love being part of what God is doing."[2] That's the spirit of these politics. And even when there are victories, there will still be work left undone to which God's Spirit calls us.

King's Ten Commandments also show the value of what Walter Fluker calls "subversive civility." Civility is important in politics because it enables us to talk and work with people different from us. It's vital to loving our neighbors because we have difficult neighbors as well as friendly ones. But civility can also be harmful. In King's day, White civility meant tiptoeing around those who supported White supremacy, making only modest reforms for fear of rocking the boat. Such was the perspective of the liberal White pastors to whom King wrote his "Letter from Birmingham City Jail." King practiced a different kind of civility, as shown in the Ten Commandments of Nonviolence. Refraining from violence with one's enemies, respecting ordinary rules of courtesy with them, praying that all might be free—these together shaped subversive civility and thereby reconfigured the very notion of public civility.[3]

In local churches I've worked with many people who practice subversive civility. I remember one who began work on our outreach committee and, after a few months, asked to meet with me. He felt some of our outreach work carried a sense of remote munificence, giving to others at a distance through other organizations. Rather than being aloof and patronizing, we should get involved with our neighbors' struggles with poverty, he said. In earlier committee meetings, he had expressed similar sentiments, yet always in a way that didn't insult or denigrate other committee members. He could express disagreement in a highly nuanced way, sometimes establishing smaller points of commonality and agreement with his opponents before expressing an overall contrary view. When he and I met and talked in more detail, I realized how respectful he had been toward people he disagreed with. Our meeting soon turned to strategy—I was happy to have an ally—as we identified existing ministries with a more attentive approach to poverty and discussed ways to bolster these ministries. Because he had been so diligent in treating committee members with respect, over the next few months many came to agree with him such that our community ministries began to reshape in focus. While this example is far less vivid and conflictual than civil rights activists dealing with White supremacists, both show subversive civility in their commitment to nonviolent speech and action, in their ultimate desire to persuade their opponents, and in their strategy that prioritizes justice and reconciliation over immediate victories.

Whether in church politics, town or city politics, or state politics, such strategies build interdependence amid the inevitable difficulties and disappointments that come alongside human beings living in community. When we see our churches as political entities, it helps us recognize Jesus's own political acumen and to use it ourselves when building communities of love and justice. Churches are public things that can be bearers of healing and good news.

11

Really? The Church?

Despite all this talk about good news in church politics, churches also disappoint us. Sometimes they do not seem like places of good news but places where human beings hurt one another in the name of God. The challenge is not simply that churches cause sin and harm, though, for any institution does that. The challenge is that churches struggle to speak truthfully about their sins and fail to confront them. We avoid repentance while claiming that it's central to Christian identity. Yet repentance can proclaim good news, and we should not avoid it. Churches can model how institutions face their sins, make restitution, and seek healing. Repentance becomes a political practice vital to a church's self-identity.

The congregants of Memorial Episcopal Church in Baltimore know about confronting their church's sins and the centrality of repentance. Their deacon, Natalie Conway, and her family had been researching family history, and one day the deacon's brother told her that someone named Charles Ridgely Howard may have enslaved their ancestors. "I was like, 'Where have I seen that name? I've seen that name,'" she said. "And sure enough, it was on one of the plaques at the back of the church." It was the name of the founding pastor. Another member of the church named Steve Howard is himself an indirect descendant of Charles Ridgely Howard. "The convergence of Conway's and Howard's stories—one arising from people enslaved at Hampton, the other from the planter class enriched by stolen human labor—became the narrative linchpin for Memorial Church's reparations work," writes journalist Cynthia Greenlee.[1] Through facing the struggle of its own history, the congregation now leads multiple efforts of racial healing in its neighborhood.

Memorial sees its work as a form of repentance and repair. The church began a reparations program that has reshaped the congregation's identity and its connections with neighbors. These reparations include a half-million-dollar fund that supports Black-led nonprofits in Baltimore, a new congregational standing committee on racial justice, and stronger ties with a Black Episcopal church nearby. It also continues to explore the underside of its history. It found, for example, that the congregation refused a major grant from the diocese in the mid-1950s because of the grant stipulations. This expansion grant, Greenlee writes, required that "the congregation would have to admit Black members. The vestry voted no and showed the rector the door."[2] It was only through facing its history squarely that the congregation has found ways to faithfully respond in the present.

Memorial's story is stark and its struggle writ large. For many churches, their struggles for repentance may not be as vivid, but they are no less real. Sometimes they take some digging to discover, other times not. Sometimes the discoveries are surprising, but in my experience that's rarely the case since the sins fit within the known history of the church.

The first step in confronting and facing sins in church politics is to recognize them. This sounds obvious, but churches have a habit of avoiding their sins. At Memorial, Steve Howard spoke about how his family previously handled knowledge that his ancestors enslaved other people. They didn't hide it, he said: "It just wasn't dwelled upon in our family history. . . . It was, 'Here were these people; they had a farm, they were involved in politics and building the city and all that—and they had slaves, too. . . . Let's move on.'"[3] Churches often handle their sins similarly. If they're not swept under the rug, they're recalled but not faced. After all, churches are generally nonconfrontational places, communities where people go to find respite from the troubles and difficulties of life elsewhere. Yet peace is not the lack of confrontation and struggle; peace involves facing confrontation and struggle knowing that wounds from past sins can be healed. Christian history is long enough for us to know that avoiding our past sins does not make them go away. That history is also long enough for us to know that hiding our sins deeply harms the church's witness to society. Sins we avoid will return to us, but those we face can be healed.

Churches face sins both large and small in our internal politics. News media focuses on big stories such as churches hiding sexual abuse scandals, with clergy covering for one another while ignoring or blaming victims. While these stories dominate the news, churches also face mundane sins that disillusion us and do not make headlines. When it comes to human resources, for example, church leaders have little training, which is often apparent during times of conflict. Rather than facing human-resource matters early in an employee's tenure, church leaders might wait until it is far too late, leaving an employee feeling as if no one ever told them that they were not performing as employers expected. Or sometimes churches will avoid confronting a member who actively harms others in the community because they fear conflict. Or church leaders use their authority as paternalism to avoid hearing important critiques from others. Churches will even exploit their government exemptions, avoiding laws that would otherwise hold them accountable. The deep sadness here is that an institution tasked with caring for vulnerable people, spreading neighbor love, and proclaiming God's justice struggles to be any more virtuous than secular institutions.

To recognize our own sins, churches might try something like the spiritual practice of examen, yet oriented to our social life. Examen is a spiritual exercise in which one takes stock of one's day, remembering moments when one felt particularly close to or far from the Holy Spirit's work. A church can do something similar. It could examine its history, remembering times when it seemed the Spirit was particularly active in its congregational life and times when the Spirit seemed distant. Here it is important to recognize that a church is always part of a larger cultural ecosystem, such that the social sins that surround it have likely seeped into its own life too.

In recognizing a congregation's broader social sins, for example, a predominantly White congregation in the United States could go through something like an examen on White supremacy, much like the process of Memorial in Baltimore. It would look at its history and interview the surrounding community to unearth ways that the congregation has participated in America's persistent history of racist policymaking. When taking on this communal spiritual practice, outsiders can be especially helpful because we insiders are often so ingrained in our communities that we don't notice our own sins.

Recognizing such sin leads to confession and then processes of restitution. Worship becomes a powerful venue for publicly confessing sins, speaking of that sin in a sacred space before the God who judges and heals our sins. Church communities have also found ways of marking their social sins outside traditional worship spaces. Some have carried out a Stations of the Cross service across their city, with various stations situated at points of sorrow—its slave market, its city hall that once passed racist legislation and might still. In Durham, North Carolina, and other cities, people have formed pilgrimages to sites of pain and hope, including places of deep sorrow and places where social movements took shape during struggles for love and justice.

The next step, restitution, usually remains ongoing. Here Christian communities seek to repair the harm of our sins. A White congregation seeking to make amends for its participation in American racism can join community partnerships or community organizing groups committed to racial healing. This commitment could lead to reparations initiatives or other such responses. Here we see three steps in this process of healing a church's social sins: recognizing sins, confessing sins, and making amends. Various wrongdoings would call for differing responses. The public response of a church whose members misappropriated church funds would be very different from one that actively avoided participating in the civil rights movement.

Repentance becomes a form of politics proclaiming a God who heals human beings amid our sins. Outsiders to the church are not necessarily surprised when the church sins, since all humans and all institutions do that. What can be heartening and uplifting is when churches have the courage to face squarely our past and present wrongdoings, refusing to hide them away and instead seeking restitution and healing. Doing this work publicly—yet not in a showy fashion—can become central to a church's wider community witness as it models how to face the consequences of social sins.

Such work can be difficult because it stirs the pot. It brings skeletons out of the closet that many would prefer remain in the dark. It can bring division because naming sins can threaten people's sense of community and long-held values. We'll see sides of people that we'd rather not see. Families who have been part of a church for generations might discover things about grandparents or great-grandparents that they'd rather not acknowledge. On the other hand, sometimes these descendants have led the charge for repentance as a way of seeking atonement. The community's narrative of itself will change. The seminary where I teach, for example, was founded by Bishop William Meade, a proponent of slavery. Our seminary is still recognizing the ways that a founder's racist vision became embedded in an institution's culture and remains there long after sins like slavery. The paternalism of that founder remains an unholy ghost of my seminary two hundred years later, still present despite our earnest efforts to change it. Such work proves difficult, and some people will inevitably resist it. Yet Christian love calls us to such difficult conversations.

Amid the church's wrongs, it's worth remembering that the church has also been at the heart of many social movements that transform society. Remembering this fact gives us hope when we are tempted to despair about the church. In antiquity, churches were vital in providing for the destitute and played a pivotal role in making poverty a greater social concern in the Roman world. They pushed to end the gruesome spectacle of gladiator games. More recently, Christians were vital to movements abolishing slavery, abolishing child labor, and dismantling imperialism. In many cases Christians instigated these movements. And in many cases Christians have been on both sides of such social change, both for and against. Yet that does not take away from the fact that churches have been instrumental to efforts repairing and healing human sin; if anything,

acknowledging Christians for and against such social change con-
tributes to the ongoing effort of recognizing our sinful histories and
repairing them for a more hopeful Christianity.

Seeing repentance as a form of politics shapes churches into
places of hope amid the sins and struggles of human beings.
Churches like Memorial in Baltimore have rebuilt their sense of
identity around a vision of Christ's body as an intercultural body
rather than a racialized body. Our wrongdoing is never the last word,
for Jesus calls us to action that brings healing and hope.

12

Finitude and Sin

We all know how our churches have disappointed us. Politics can be one of the most disappointing parts of church life, and so it's important to get to the root of that disappointment. We often associate our disappointment with someone sinning—and often somebody else, not us!—but our disappointment doesn't always relate to sin. Sometimes our disappointment relates to the ordinary difficulties of living in human community. Disappointment sometimes comes from our limitation as humans—our finitude—rather than from sinful acts. Knowing that difference can help us face our disappointments. And even when we do face outright sin in church politics, Christian tradition gives us models for how to heal when we sin against each other.

Getting clear about the differences between finitude and sin can help us navigate our responses to disappointment. Take, for example, a church that has remodeled its worship space, and church leadership decides to move the choir. The move excites some people in the congregation but upsets others. It's difficult to say that moving a choir is an immoral act, at least in normal circumstances, and so it wouldn't fit into the category of sin. Sin means missing the mark of God's good intentions of love and justice, whether that sin comes from an act we carry out ourselves or from something we fail to do (those are sins of commission versus sins of omission). Disappointment from moving the choir relates to finitude, not sin. A change in worship space opens up new opportunities but closes off others. There are not limitless options regarding where the choir goes, and any decision is likely to disappoint someone. Finitude simply relates to humans having limits and boundaries in the world we live in. Those limits can feel greater in a community setting since we are facing the limits of multiple people and of multiple circumstances.

We confuse finitude and sin for good reason. Both can lead to disappointment with other people. They also get tangled together sometimes: in difficult circumstances, our finitude can lead to situations in which we have no choice but to choose between two wrongs. That is, our finitude can lead to sin. In some of those cases, it wasn't our own choices that brought us to a sinful decision but the fact that we ended up facing two bad options. And sometimes we do not know in the moment whether we are facing an outright sin or whether we are simply facing a situation that confronts our finitude. Theologians like Augustine and John Calvin have pointed out that our finitude means that we do not have the ability to see sin clearly. Realizing how finitude and sin are distinguished as well as how they sometimes overlap helps us confront our disappointment with church politics, which in turn helps us discern appropriate responses when we feel disappointed.

We face finitude in our churches in big decisions such as whether to move choir seating, but even more so in ordinary ones. If someone avoids speaking to a newcomer during coffee hour because they prefer gossiping with their clique, this rejection of a newcomer comes from direct wrongdoing, from sin. But what if someone sees a newcomer, yet she's already in a conversation with a grieving friend who just lost his mother? Caring for this grieving person by listening intently might mean not greeting the newcomer. The newcomer could reasonably feel lonely in this situation and wonder how well this church welcomes visitors. Similarly, if many people wish to serve on a church board but there are limited spots, those who are excluded may feel hurt. They have reason to feel hurt, regardless of whether the board is decided by vote, by lot, or otherwise. No one committed a direct wrong in this situation; rather, the struggle emerged from human finitude, in this case a reasonable limit in the number of positions on a board. In my own ministry, difficulties related to finitude can feel harder to navigate than those related to sin because in cases of obvious wrongdoing the response can seem clearer. Responses to finitude feel fuzzier.

With finitude, our congregations should learn from wider politics. In city and state politics, we have a more intuitive understanding of finitude. We recognize that a city's budget is too small to meet all the needs of that city. No one has sinned in many such situations; it's a challenge of competing goods. In our congregations it can be harder to accept such limits because we expect a level of personal spiritual solace from our churches that we don't expect in our wider political life. But such disappointment is natural to any human community. Generosity toward others in the face of such disappointment bolsters our politics of interdependence.

It's important to say that finitude isn't harmful or bad; rather, it's part of the created goodness of this world. Since finitude often leads to disappointment and since we can confuse it with sin, the goodness of our finitude can be hard to see, much less accept. As humans we sometimes fight our finitude, wishing that we could remove the limits we face. Yet God made us with finitude and called that good. Accepting and embracing finitude is part of wise and faithful Christian living, since appreciating it leads directly to recognizing interconnection and interdependence. My finitude means that I depend on others, that I can't live life on my own. I need others and they need me. While finitude prevented someone from offering hospitality to a newcomer, in a church characterized by interdependence someone else would welcome this visitor and make them feel at home. Appreciating finitude enables us to embrace the love, mutuality, and vulnerability of human life.

Church leaders should speak openly about their finitude and disappointments. Pastoral leaders openly discussing their limitations helps establish a church that values vulnerability and recognizes how every person in the community needs others. Church leaders can set expectations about projects that can be done only as a community. Recognizing our finitude moves us away from hero ministry, that tendency for individuals to take on more and more in hopes that their extra effort will save the church. Instead, we can see that any thriving ministry requires mutuality. In an outreach ministry, for example, recognizing finitude can enable a church community to identify not only what it can do in its surrounding community but also what it can't do. No single congregation or nonprofit can end hunger in its city or make expensive housing affordable; it has to collaborate with others. Doing outreach ministries in a way that is mindful of our finitude and interdependence can also help cut off the paternalism that often pervades Christian outreach ministry. Instead of thinking that our congregation can solve a problem, we recognize that we need the gifts and abilities of others—most especially those we claim to be serving. Rather than hindering ministry, recognizing finitude can expand our ministries by deepening our ability to cooperate.

Other times, however, our church conflicts involve outright sin. And sometimes sin pervades all sides of a church conflict. In our sin, churches can engage in violence even if we do not go to war with each other. We may not use swords or guns, but we are violent with our words, our hearts, and our lawsuits. During such conflicts—church property disputes are a common one—we should recognize that we are usually engaged in and with human sin. If we are harming other parties and going to court, we are already beyond the bounds of commended Christian behavior, as when the apostle Paul tells Christians not to take each other to court (1 Cor 6:1–8). A difficulty of this life is that sometimes Christians will have conflicts so deep that we end up in places like courts. It's tempting to think that there is some way to act without sinning during such times, and perhaps there is. More often, however, I've seen this temptation lead to self-righteousness. I've sat in large church gatherings where discussion of taking an opponent to court led to standing ovations, as if we were flawless and our opponent vicious. It seems better to recognize that we are probably sinning during these times—or at least recognize that we are engaged in sinful matters as sinful people such that our sin is surely getting mixed up in the situation.

Here there are salient lessons from the Christian just war tradition, checkered as that tradition has been. The just war tradition recognizes the sorrow that takes place in war and its impact on soldiers. The tradition asks combatants to do difficult things. It not only asks soldiers to harm and sometimes kill combatants but it also asks them to do this while recognizing that one's enemy is a child of God. It recognizes that soldiers are involved in harmful and sinful activity, and it asks soldiers to seek God's forgiveness for what they have done. In the rhetoric of war, it would seem easier to vilify the enemy, to glorify the rightness of one's cause, and to say that others are getting what they deserve. But the just war tradition, at its best, sees differently. It has a more realistic human psychology than one that vilifies the other, for we cannot harm or kill others without such actions harming ourselves.

Activity like warfare or a church property dispute takes a toll on our spirits. In property disputes, keeping a congregation from worshiping in their usual space because they've left the denomination harms that congregation. They've been left without a place to worship God. Amid this fact, the larger judicatory body may have justifiable reasons for retaining that property. In most instances I know of in my own Episcopal Church, by canon law the land is held by the diocese rather than the local congregation. In the heated atmosphere of property disputes, I've seen such congregations demonize their judicatory in inaccurate and slanderous ways, and I've seen judicatories demonize such congregations. It aids the souls in all parties to recognize that all are participating in sin here.

In parts of the medieval just war tradition, soldiers returning from war were required to go to confession before participating in the wider worshiping community. Such a requirement recognized the harm, the hurt, and the trauma of warfare. It recognized that one could hardly participate in war without sinning in some way. Similarly, church disputes carry their wounds into our souls. Recognizing and confessing such sins is a first step in healing these wounds in ourselves, in our communities, and in the community we call our enemy.

At this point it's worth returning to Augustine and his account of sin. Sin is misdirected and disordered love—a statement both realistic and hopeful. For Augustine, human beings take the good things that God has created and use them for wrong. Behind any wrong that humans commit, deep down lies some kind of love being misused. Ignoring someone during a church coffee hour just because we prefer to talk to known acquaintances excludes the newcomer. In doing so we misdirect our love. We love our community as it is instead of as it could be, and so we refuse to welcome someone. Church coffee hour seems like a mild example, but that same instinct of loving our community as it is instead of being open to neighbors proves to be at the root of plenty of social sins in our churches.

Amid churches' flaws, the idea that sins are misdirected loves gives hope. Even amid sin, loving interdependence is not out of reach because such sin is still based in a desire to love. And if a sin is based in love, then our sin is not beyond healing. Churchgoers can greet people at coffee hour because they imagine their community as a place of loving welcome.

There is an old saying, "Church politics are the worst politics." I suspect that we say this because we expect more out of church politics than secular politics, and rightly so. Yet I remain hopeful. I don't think they're the worst politics, for when churches' internal politics are working modestly well, it's still a hopeful place. I recall a pastor in my diocese responding to someone complaining about church politics. The pastor said, "Sure there are politics in this diocese. But what's different is that I know most of the players. I can call them on the phone and we can talk. And if we're all starting with love, then that's a different kind of politics. That gives me hope." It is a modest hope because the church is a body populated by flawed human beings. Yet it's also an eternal hope because God's Spirit indwells our flawed humanity and our politics.

13

Authority and Leadership

Any human community, even the most egalitarian, has structures of authority. Think back to the once-trendy "flat hierarchy" workplaces. While they avoided formal structures as a way of sidestepping hierarchies, they simply ended up with informal means of authority. The idea of no supervisors and choosing your projects might sound appealing, but for many employees it felt terrible. Their workplace still had power players but with fewer restrictions on how they behaved. The power players took advantage of the system, ignoring highly capable employees just because they didn't want to work with them. Work felt "a lot like high school," one employee said.[1] Avoiding hierarchies and authority altogether won't help us since that usually leads to more pernicious forms of authority. Any politics involves authority of some kind, as some people make decisions that other people have to live with.

Yet Christian Scriptures also voice clear egalitarian commitments. We find these in Paul's image of the interdependent body of Christ and in Jesus's teaching before his death, discussed shortly. So how do we navigate balancing the church's egalitarian commitments with necessary structures of authority? Authority and interdependence should be seen in fruitful tension instead of in opposition. Rather than exerting authority by expecting or demanding submission, church leaders can employ authority to bolster loving interdependence. As with Jesus in the Gospels, authority can take different expressions in different circumstances, all for the purpose of spreading God's love and justice. This is leadership that does not dominate and does not resort to violence but rather builds interdependence.

Jesus's words and actions in the upper room before his crucifixion again provide paradigmatic guidance from the New Testament.

Jesus gathers a group of leaders—his disciples—who are shaping the movement he began and will shape it even more profoundly after his death, resurrection, and ascension. Earlier I noted how this moment carries significant political importance in the New Testament: not only is Jesus about to be crucified as a political prisoner, but now he tells his disciples how to order their own politics as church community. He tells them about authority in the kingdom of God. Recall Luke 22:24: "[Jesus] said to them, 'The kings of the gentiles lord it over them, and those in authority over them are called benefactors. But not so with you; rather, the greatest among you must become like the youngest and the leader like one who serves.'" The disciples, of course, had just been arguing among themselves about who was the greatest. Jesus does not rebuke the disciples sternly; instead, he simply tells them that they sound like gentile kings who flaunt their authority.

Jesus does not dwell on these kings, but the contrast is clear enough. They glory in their power over others. By that understanding, one person's greatness comes at the expense of another's. Authority rooted in divine power, on the other hand, does not glory in overcoming or dominating. The primary mark of power rooted in divinity is humility. Such power does not revel in itself but gladly shares power with others. As Jesus shares his power in the Gospels, his own power does not diminish but increases. Think of Luke 10, in which Jesus sends out seventy-two followers who preach and heal in the towns Jesus will visit. As Jesus spreads power among them, his power grows too. In some human calculations power and authority appear a zero-sum game. One person having power means others must not, and so those with power flaunt it. But for Jesus, sharing and distributing power only extends his own divine power.

Jesus expressly tells his disciples to act similarly. Greatness and leadership entail sharing power, holding it lightly, and being willing to move to different places of status in varying circumstances. "The greatest among you must become like the youngest and the leader like one who serves." We see Jesus's understanding of the need for flexible authority on full display in John. In John's portrayal of the upper room, Jesus enacts this understanding of authority by washing his disciples' feet. One moment he acts as a servant to his disciples; the next he returns to the role of teacher as he gives the upper-room discourse in John 14–17. Jesus willingly takes on varying roles that carry completely different connotations of status. In one moment he acts as a servant; in the next moment he acts as a revered teacher.[2]

Notice that Jesus neither denies the role of power, authority, and status nor gives it deference. In Luke 22, he makes mention of the gentile rulers but quickly moves on, such that these secular leaders do not greatly concern Jesus. In his own ministry, Jesus often seems playful with his authority. When political and religious leaders like scribes and Pharisees challenge him, Jesus employs his own power and authority as a popular and revered religious teacher to sternly rebuke them (Mark 12:24–27). In contrast, when Jesus encounters people who seem to carry little power, his manner transforms into gentle meekness, as when he publicly offers grace to the woman caught in adultery (John 8:2–11). The disciples carry on this playfulness with authority and gentleness in the book of Acts. When Sadducees arrest Peter and he subsequently speaks before "rulers, elders, and scribes assembled in Jerusalem"—a powerful gathering, to be sure—he whimsically retorts that he has been arrested "because of a good deed" (Acts 4:5–9). A few chapters later, Peter quietly and gently prays alone by the bedside of Tabitha and resurrects her from the dead (Acts 9:36–43). When around the politically powerful, Jesus and the disciples act artfully with the authority they have. This shows political savviness combined with a conviction that they do not take earthly political power too seriously. To those who have little worldly authority, Jesus consistently shows gentleness and mercy.

In the upper room, then, Jesus does not tell his disciples that there is no power and authority in the kingdom of God; instead, Jesus reorients those terms. Power and authority are expressed in humility by lifting others up. Power and authority rightly used in the reign of God enable and increase our interdependence.

Jesus's words and actions in the upper room have led to the notion of servant leadership. Such leadership does not mean constantly deferring to others and never asserting oneself—that is certainly not how Jesus behaves in the Gospels. Jesus rarely defers to scribes and Pharisees nor even to his disciples. A servant leader recognizes their own dependence upon God and interdependence with others. Sometimes this entails sharing power and letting others lead; sometimes it entails harnessing one's power to spread love in a particular moment. Any seasoned pastor knows, for example, that they can harness their authority as a spiritual leader to change the course of a harmful group conversation by interjecting and using their authority rightly. Such assertive power builds up the community since it's rarely helpful to be deferential in such circumstances. Such assured leadership increases interdependence because some are actively harming others. Servant leadership does not erase the self; it intensifies a leader's selfhood and builds interdependent community. It is empowering rather than paternalizing.

Jesus also had a remarkable ability to adapt to cultural systems around him while at the same time prophetically challenging injustices within them. Similarly, Christian leaders should recognize the varied and complex systems of which we are a part—systems as big as our global economy and as small as our congregations and church boards—without being overtaken by their centrifugal force. If we do not do interior work with the Holy Spirit, leaders simply replicate sinful habits of the systems in which we find ourselves. Here again human communities seek stasis, which pushes leaders to uphold that stasis even if it proves harmful. Leading amid the push and pull of these systems necessitates nurturing our connection with the eternal life given to us by the Spirit, such that the Spirit's work becomes our anchor amid turmoil. A deeply grounded spiritual life provides courage and additional perspective to face sinful habits in our systems. Christian leadership grounded in the Spirit can harness the Spirit's power to lift up the downtrodden and humble the mighty.

A final pitfall Christian leaders face is the capacity for paternalism within ordained ministry. One of the greatest gifts of ministry is that of encouragement, helping people see who they are and who they might become. When people in our congregation tell us who they are, we have the opportunity to name the holy and the good in their lives, to help them see parts of themselves that they have not emphasized or seen. This is a position of great spiritual authority, one to both cherish and hold lightly. This kind of authority has the capacity to give life and to go terribly wrong. Telling people who they are quickly turns into paternalism when it drifts away from showing people how they are beloved of God and instead moves to something that perpetuates a pastor's own harmful frameworks of identity, such as a pastor who dismisses a queer person's narration of themselves. On the other hand, when a pastor responds to that story with care and identifies how God's love is the source of how they love, then a pastor can participate in bringing new life to someone who has been told that their love doesn't fit in church.

To continue Augustine's theme of sin as misdirected good, the good of encouragement can become distorted into sinful paternalism. In ministry we cannot tell people who they are without *them*, that is, without encountering them, hearing them, and recognizing them. There are times when a pastoral encounter with another person upends our assumptions—pastors should reflect carefully about how such encounters should change us and perhaps alter our own values. Ultimately it is not the pastor who says who someone is. God creates, redeems, and sustains each of us. This pastoral side of ministry, done well, can have profound political consequences for a community. When a pastor truly hears someone, that connection between pastor and congregant builds deep relationships and allows them to do more work in their community than they could without that trust and connection.

In sum, pastors have a strange kind of authority—one of nonviolent, nonmanipulative, and nondominating leadership. Put positively, it is authority grounded in loving interdependence and peace. At times it feels that pastors do not possess a great deal of authority compared with other political leaders; I've often felt that way as a pastor. We do not, after all, have anything like the coercive power of physical force like the gentile kings of whom Jesus spoke. Nor do we even have the power of a teacher wielding a grade. The power of preaching, presiding at services, setting meeting agendas, and the day-to-day work of administering a church can seem like small-scale power. Instead of regretting that we don't have more power, we can recognize the good of such limitations to our authority, both for our communities and for our souls. Rather than wielding power through violence, at our best we wield power through persuasion. It is vital to Christian authority and leadership.[3] Such persuasion is grounded in a love that recognizes our interdependence, for it refuses to force its own way and recognizes our connection with one another.

Questions for Reflection and Discussion for Part 3

- What do ordinary meetings look like in your congregation?
  What kind of politics do they cultivate?
- What sorts of sins do you see in the church that need healing?
  How can your congregation participate in that healing?
- When has the difference between sin and finitude seemed
  unclear in your church life?
- When have you encountered leaders who embody the qualities
  described in chapter 13? What about their character and their
  actions made them a good leader?

Recommended Reading for Part 3

Fluker, Walter Earl. *Ethical Leadership: The Quest for Character, Civility,
and Community.* Philadelphia: Fortress, 2009.

St. Gregory the Great. *The Book of Pastoral Rule.* Translated by George
Demacopoulos. Crestwood, NY: St. Vladimir's, 2007.

PART 4

The Firstfruits of Public Life

14

The Congregation in the Wider Community

We now move to ways that congregations relate to wider politics of towns, cities, states, and nation-states. As a church loves its neighbors, it should find itself engaged in local politics in ways that change both the neighborhood and the church. That's because faithfully following Jesus means a church welcomes neighbors into its life, whether neighbors join its worship, enjoy its fellowship, or simply use its buildings. Following Jesus also means that a congregation sees neighbors who suffer. In doing so, it will find injustices within its community. Facing such injustices will then involve the church in matters of local town or city politics.

Yet when it comes to engaging politics, it is tempting for churches to bypass their neighborhoods and move directly to national issues. These issues, after all, garner a great deal of attention. When churches jump to national politics without engaging local politics, however, their work gets abstracted from a congregation's own life. Say a church sends a group of congregants to a protest, especially when protests are happening across the country. Such engagement can be quite appropriate, but if the work stops there, then the work lacks roots. The church could be part of these protests while also probing its own life and seeing how its history and identity might still perpetuate the thing they're protesting.

It's similarly tempting to identify our nation with Christianity, imagining the United States or anywhere else as a Christian nation blessed by God in ways other nations aren't. There has been enough sin enacting by so-called Christian nations, however, to make us cautious about the idea. The church has been around a long time, long enough to see many nations call themselves Christian while acting in morally abhorrent ways—persecuting religious minorities, waging war in the name of Christianity, settling on other people's land while calling it their own, all while imagining that these activities help Christianity. After all the sins enacted in the name of Christian nations, the idea now seems like a failure of political imagination.

The idea also limits politics to statecraft. We can see why the idea is tempting: we want Christianity to shape our politics, we associate politics with statecraft, and then we assume that the primary way to express Christian politics is to promote a Christian nation. Yet we should remember the way of Jesus. He was not a crony of the Roman Empire but was killed by it for preaching a message of nonviolent love. The idea of a Christian nation conflates Christianity and politics with nationhood and statecraft, thereby compromising the church's witness.

Another pitfall of moving directly to national issues is that a church risks being co-opted for partisan purposes. Without the rootedness that local politics requires, church communities can be tempted by the lures of power that accompany national partisan politics. After all, partisan politicians covet the access to constituents that any congregation offers. Christians take our weekly worship for granted sometimes, but gathering a community of constituents on a weekly basis without having to do major outreach campaigns to bring people together is an enviable thing in politics. When church communities become co-opted for partisan aims, we waver from our singular focus on the gospel of Jesus and his call of neighbor love. When rooted locally, however, churches gain discernment about local matters, which can subsequently inform careful engagement with national issues.

Being prudent about partisan politics doesn't mean that a congregation should actively avoid everything that may appear partisan, however. If a mayor wants to visit a church, there is nothing wrong with welcoming her. Its leaders should simply be cognizant of the fact that the politician has her own aims in visiting and set up the event accordingly. The church should remain ever cautious, after all, for political parties can manipulate the moral credibility that churches provide. Neither should a church avoid a political issue simply because one political party is for it and another against it. If political parties have different views on refugees who fled into the nation, this should not mean a congregation should avoid the moral question of how it treats refugees in its community. Neither does supporting refugees in this case imply wholesale support for one party over another. One party will probably say the church is meddling, while another may make something of the church's support for refugees. None of this should be surprising to churches, nor should it inhibit the church from its work with refugees.[1]

In congregations it's simply healthier to start locally. Beginning locally does not mean avoiding the conflict and bitterness of national politics—far from it. I've often found that the vitriol of local politics proves worse than national politics, as all civility gets lost when it comes to people's neighborhoods. We can expect that kind of conflict in local politics without losing heart about our political engagement.

How then should a congregation determine where to begin engaging public life in its community? We start by asking the simple question, *What is going on?* What is happening in this community? Who is suffering? What injustices are taking place?

One important entry point involves listening carefully to strangers who come to our church. If a congregation has a ministry to those who are hungry, its leaders should take notice of their encounters. Do people who are hungry tend to come from certain neighborhoods nearby? Why those neighborhoods and not others? What are the demographic trends regarding who is hungry? Why are the demographics of hunger skewed toward some populations and not others? A little extra research goes a long way in addressing these questions. While research on a national scale can provide context, it is vital to examine local circumstances, which usually entails digging into a region's history. If many people seeking assistance come from a particular neighborhood, then find out the history of that neighborhood and those around it. One will usually find town or city policies that led to some neighborhoods having more wealth than others. Where I grew up in Richmond, Virginia, for example, one would find things like "urban renewal" programs from the mid- to late twentieth century that declared certain neighborhoods blighted—often prosperous Black neighborhoods—and said these programs would improve them even though they often increased poverty.

In one of my congregations, we noticed demographic trends of our hunger ministry and began to do neighborhood-based research. This led to two responses. First, we organized with other churches to start a new emergency assistance program in another neighborhood, since poverty had lessened in our neighborhood but increased in others. Second, we began advocating for housing affordability since most people coming for food assistance were spending well over half of their income on rent payments—far more than just a few years before, and well over the general guideline of spending around one-third of one's income on housing. As housing prices skyrocketed in our city, more people were going hungry.

We did not portray housing affordability as a national partisan issue to our congregation, largely because it wasn't one. We cast housing affordability exactly how we saw it—as an issue based in our experiences with struggling neighbors who couldn't pay their rent. That bypassed partisan rancor. In this example of housing affordability—and every other one in this book from my church ministry—we had people from both sides of the political aisle joining together in local issues. Local politics finds alliances we wouldn't expect in national politics, after all, like Republicans and progressive Democrats agreeing to zoning changes that use the market economy to address housing affordability. Focusing on people and issues rather than partisan platforms helps navigate the difficulties of partisanship in congregations.

As pastors and leaders our job is to show people what is happening, to hold before them the struggle and sorrow of our city or town. Our task is to be with Jesus as he stands with those who suffer, helping our congregations respond to that suffering. As leaders we do not necessarily need to know how the congregation should immediately respond, since that is a matter for communal discernment, but we are called to expose our congregations to the hurt and hardship of our neighborhoods. Such suffering is not a partisan matter; it is a human matter, and Jesus calls us to act. Our congregations cannot forget those who suffer around us because God hasn't forgotten them.

The divine love known in our congregations can spread to our wider community. Yet also, as we engage the community, the Holy Spirit will employ that wider community to reshape our discipleship. In our churches we share interdependence with neighborhoods around us.

15

Limits of Hyperlocal Politics

Amid the importance of local politics for our churches, there are dangers that we should not overlook. Focusing exclusively on highly local matters, sometimes called a hyperlocal approach, neglects wider social sins that entangle a neighborhood and church community. It overlooks how deeply our neighborhoods and towns are entwined with one another socially, economically, and spiritually. My own neighborhood's sins are usually connected to other neighborhoods nearby, and my neighborhood's well-being depends upon others nearby.

In the United States, the interconnection of neighborhoods' sins is most evident in racist housing policy. During the mid-twentieth century, White Americans set up an apartheid-style system of housing and land ownership that ensured Black Americans and other persons of color could not own property in predominantly White neighborhoods. Property values in many White neighborhoods grew and exacerbated wealth disparities in the United States. Churches were hardly exempt from this movement; rather, they were part of it. We see it in the geography of newly established White churches during the 1940s to 1960s. In many metropolitan areas across the United States, newly established churches during this era provide a basic map of White flight. It's not that White churches followed White flight—it's that they were often the first institutions established along its path. Sometimes White church leaders explicitly supported Whites-only neighborhoods, but more often they offered spiritual comfort to new congregations while ignoring the racism embedded in their new built environment. White churches did not simply benefit from White flight; they helped promote White flight in what became a period of unprecedented wealth accumulation for White Americans and White churches.[1]

In a hyperlocal approach it's very easy to overlook this history by focusing exclusively on one's own neighborhood. It could be easy for a White congregation to look around its neighborhood, notice that most people are White, and assume that its localized moral responsibilities do not involve fighting racism. In this way a hyperlocal church would promote racism because it neglects the racism built into the physical space of neighborhoods. Instead, one should ask, *Why* is my neighborhood so White? What led to this, and what is perpetuating it? The covenants and laws in place at the founding of a neighborhood, for example, carry ramifications for generations as certain neighborhoods receive more money for schools, transportation, and other public services, and these neighborhoods in turn produce and attract more wealth. Even if those covenants are no longer legally binding, their legacies remain. White and Black Americans with identical credit scores still have very different experiences securing a home loan, for example.

Nor is this challenge exclusive to suburban congregations. Plenty of predominantly White urban churches are experiencing growth today, driven partly by gentrification and growing White populations in cities. Here too it's necessary to face the institutional and historical racism associated with such a change. As theologian Willie Jennings writes, "People will not fight you at all when you say we need to learn to love each other. But if you say that the configuration of real estate must show how we love one another, they will fight you tooth and nail."² Pastors and lay leaders need not skirt the difficulties and conflicts associated with this struggle.

In my own Episcopal denomination, we value something called the Anglican "parish system" but can overlook a potential shadow side. The term "parish" may be less familiar to some, but it carries an important theological quality that links our churches with their surrounding neighborhoods. A parish includes not just those who gather on Sunday morning but the surrounding community too. In this system a parish has responsibility and obligation for all who live in its geographic area, not just its church members. It's a model that many Anglican churches turn to when engaging local politics. But for

White parishes established during White flight, valuing the parish system can lead to these same problems of hyperlocal politics. Their local community was entirely White for years, shaping an identity that did not recognize its interdependence with nearby neighborhoods. In the Catholic Church, which follows a similar system, the divides are less subtle. Black Catholic churches sometimes formed nearby White Catholic churches because of Whites who did not want to receive communion with Black Catholics. This is a deep distortion of the parish system, which seeks to bring Christians in a geographic area together amid their difference and diversity.

Similarly, in recent years I've worked with pastors leading congregations in neighborhoods going through demographic transitions whose congregations are struggling to bring in new members. Oftentimes it is a White congregation in a once predominantly White suburban neighborhood becoming a more multicultural neighborhood. Pastors have shared how their predominantly White congregations cannot seem to grow even while the surrounding neighborhood grows and changes. Even though the congregation strives to be hospitable, has ministries in the neighborhood, and has an evangelistic spirit, sometimes these churches still don't attract newcomers from the surrounding community. During prior generations, when the neighborhood grew, the church grew too. So what's different now?

In many cases, a church's overwhelmingly White identity proves so baked in that they struggle to welcome newcomers who aren't White. With the church having been established during White flight, their local demographics were White for decades. As neighborhoods changed more recently, these churches have had difficulty welcoming their neighbors because neighbors are not exclusively White anymore. Even if they speak openly about how they want a more intercultural community, in their habits they lack the cultural resources to make others feel welcome.

A Christian politics of loving interdependence, on the other hand, recognizes a church's connection with nearby neighborhoods. It recognizes that just as individuals depend upon one another for their existence and identity, so also do neighborhoods and counties. All of us are bound up with one another. Churches can both challenge the policies that have led to divided neighborhoods and also be a model of overcoming these divisions.

Oftentimes in the United States people do not go to church in their neighborhood, which raises a related set of issues. While I think there are great benefits to attending church near where we live, there are also good reasons why people do not. Where queer-affirming churches are rare, for example, people might have to drive a long way to find a church that includes them. If we drive some distance to church, one thing to remember is that we are still interconnected to our church's neighborhood and indeed to the neighborhoods we pass through to get to church. If we can drive to that church, then there are certainly social and economic networks that connect the place we live to the place we go to church. We should recognize and explore those connections.

Building networks and coalitions with other churches as well as interfaith and secular social service organizations proves one of the most effective ways to work toward healing fragmented neighborhoods, whether we drive long distances to church or whether we're trying to build interconnections across distant neighborhoods. Coalitions between churches enable us to encounter one another amid the disparate nature of so many American cities and towns, given how spread out many metropolitan areas can be.[3] Without such encounters, churches risk mimicking an American consumerism in which products—in this case spiritual products—are disconnected from place and geography.

Such coalitions can be means of facing and undoing legacies like housing apartheid in the United States. In my hometown of Richmond, Virginia, for example, a group of churches recognized the challenge of separated neighborhoods and started looking for ways to combat it. They realized that, in their context, neighborhoods became isolated from one another in part because there wasn't a strong transit system to connect them. The existing transit system didn't provide strong connections between financial centers and lower-income neighborhoods, which exacerbated wealth disparities in the city.[4] Lack of public transportation also prevented building relationships across racial lines due to the Richmond area's history of segregated neighborhoods. So churches banded together during the 2010s to advocate for rapid transit service across various parts of the city, led by Richmond Hill, the interracial monastic-styled community noted earlier. A few years later Richmond opened its first bus rapid transit service, with a 17 percent increase in public transit ridership in the first year of operation, as people had a safe and effective means of getting to and from work or elsewhere.

The nature of local politics means that churches' proposals in public matters like this one have a conditional quality. Once a congregation has explored the question of what is going on, the responses will vary dramatically from place to place. In the case of rapid transit services, skeptics retorted that a bus service does not necessarily seem like something "Christian" per se. Jesus makes no mention of buses in the New Testament, after all. But this misses the point. Since every community is different, Jesus's universal commandment to love our neighbors means that love will take different shapes and forms in different places. It might even appear strange to those who live well outside that community. Engaging neighborhood life will look very different for a church in a densely populated urban area compared to a church in a lightly populated small town. When responding to different situations, judgments will have a "fluid and flexible character," in theologian Kathryn Tanner's words.[5] Jesus's political culture in the first century is not our culture, and so our politics should look different, while still inspired by Jesus's commandment to love our neighbors.

Hyperlocal politics can be a pernicious form of local politics if it seeks the perceived welfare of its own neighborhood at the expense of surrounding neighborhoods. Churches either participate in such harmful politics or become communities embodying interdependence by recognizing how our neighborhoods rely on each other. Building relationships with each other across churches then becomes a vital means of shaping towns and cities that recognize and enact their interdependence. Here, too, churches can be leaven in the loaf of public life.

16

Seeking the Welfare of the City

As churches engage wider politics of their town or city, it helps to have a framework for thinking about the church's life in relation to these governing authorities. One of the most enduring frameworks in Christian tradition comes from Augustine, inspired by the prophet Jeremiah.

When Israelites were taken captive by the Babylonians in 597 BC, Jeremiah spoke carefully to them. Their entire way of life had been upended, including the relation between their political life and religious life. Previously their religious life had been entwined with their homeland. However much prophets and kings argued with one another, they were both still part of the people of Israel living in the land of Judah. They were now entering a new environment, oppressed under foreign rule while still worshipping YHWH.

What did Jeremiah tell them amid this dizzying new religious and political reality? Given the trauma of conquest and exile, surely it would have been tempting to tell the exiles in Babylon to try their hand at a revolt, to blow up the system from the inside. Another temptation would be to tell the Israelites to isolate themselves, securing their own holiness without much regard for the unholy city of Babylon. But Jeremiah said something else. Jeremiah's prophecy told the Israelites to build a life there: "Build houses and live in them; plant gardens and eat what they produce." They should marry and have children. Overall, Jeremiah's prophecy said, "seek the welfare of the city where I have sent you into exile, and pray to the Lord on its behalf, for in its welfare you will find your welfare" (Jer 29:5–7).

Jeremiah provided a model for Israel's faithfulness amid exile, away from the towns and cities of Israel that provided the cohesive religious community they were used to. Jeremiah recognized that, difficult as exile was, the exiles' spiritual life was caught up in Babylon's life. Seeking the welfare of their city became a spiritual practice. God called Israel to witness to the living God in a strange land, to stay faithful amid their exile.

Jeremiah shows another deep spiritual lesson, that the life of the city or community in which we live shapes our spirits. Cities are physical places, but they are also spiritual entities that shape human life in distinct ways. Some features of a city build up our spirits, while others harm our spirits. The Israelites were interdependent with the city of their exile. This interdependence did not mean deference to that city and its authorities—as the book of Daniel shows, exiles could challenge Babylonian authorities with courage and cleverness. Jeremiah provides a model for forming a common life and recognizing the spirituality of that common life in contexts where neighbors do not share the same religious commitments, that is, what we now call religious pluralism.

Augustine takes Jeremiah's prophecy as a paradigm for understanding Christian political life during this world, during the time before God's final redemption of creation.[1] Christians live among and between two societies, the earthly city and the new Jerusalem. Both cities are communities founded on what its people love. The earthly city is built on misdirected love, while the new Jerusalem is built on love of God. Earthly cities are the political regimes and orders of this world. They come and go; they exist in history but not eternally. This does not mean earthly cities are evil—on the contrary, their existence constitutes part of the goodness of God's creation. Christians are citizens of their earthly cities and find their own welfare in the welfare of these cities. Yet Christians are also—and more so—citizens of the new Jerusalem. The new Jerusalem is another society, one that exists in this world and exists more fully in the world to come. It is an eternal community of saints, a heavenly city that interpenetrates our life today. We are part of both cities. Both cities shape us.

Given my emphasis on church life, it's important to say that Augustine does not neatly align the new Jerusalem with the church. Augustine is not distinguishing between church and state in his talk of two cities. The church contains both saints and sinners—as our individual selves contain sainthood and sinfulness. The church is part of the earthly city. Certainly the Spirit uses the church as witness to the living Christ, but Augustine does not equate the church with God's own political work in the world in a simplistic fashion. Thus Augustine provides an important caution. Congregations are holy places but are not the sole means of God's work in the world and can themselves be deeply flawed. The congregation is not the kingdom of God; it too is a mixed community.

Augustine's framework helps us in several ways. First, he values earthly political identities, like that of our city or country, without giving them undue spiritual power or authority. Augustine sounds hard on the earthly city at times, but he's simply saying that the earthly city is neither a purely divine order nor utterly depraved and corrupt. He relativizes the earthly city. No earthly city or party within that city will be so divinely inspired that it should receive the wholesale support of the church. Nor is any party within the church a flawless representation of the heavenly city. Earthly cities will always have their flaws and injustices. Yet the fact that they will always have flaws is no reason for despair. Some cities approximate justice more ably than others. We can build better cities during this world.

With its focus on love, Augustine's framework also provides hope mixed with an appropriate realism. If humans and our societies are always striving toward love, the community life of our earthly city is still striving toward something good. It will surely focus on love of self at times, but here again it's still rooted in love even if it's distorted love. An Augustinian certainly has tempered hope about how much repair is achieved before the new Jerusalem, but human politics are never beyond repair since they are based in love.

Augustine's framework also avoids Christian sectarianism, the temptation to distinguish Christian identity to such a degree that one neglects seemingly external matters. Some Christians express sectarianism by imagining the church as the heavenly city itself, seeking refuge from the ambiguities of the earthly city. Augustine wouldn't have much room for this view since even the church is a mixed body with both saints and sinners. Whereas Augustinians find our welfare in a surrounding city's welfare, sectarianism neglects its own Christian witness by thinking it can cleanly draw lines between Christians' welfare and that of their city. Our Christian witness remains interdependent with our wider community's. Sectarianism also prevents Christians from seeing real movements of God in the politics of this world—events like the abolition of industrial child labor through nineteenth- and twentieth-century movements led by Christians. In such events God's justice truly broke into this world, and so Christians should name this work of God as such.

For some secular thinkers, the Christian emphasis on love in politics harms wider nation-state conversations because it imports the Christian value of love into public spaces. Such spaces, they say, should be neutral regarding religious values. Yet such strict neutrality seems unrealistic. It seems more reasonable to seek a plural public space rather than an areligious public space. After all, any politics involves matters that relate to human beings' values. Keeping those values completely outside public life inhibits fulsome public discourse. For Christians, we can talk about love in public without expecting that love will be a central stated value of the state—the central value will more likely be justice. Yet love and justice are entwined for Christians, and so for us to care about justice in public life we also have to care about love since we interpret justice with love. Still, we needn't necessarily ask the state to follow our Christian expression of love all the way down in a plural environment. Martin Luther King Jr. is here again paradigmatic: he led a pluralist movement for justice while his speeches and writings put love at the center of human life.

One can voice the Augustinian tradition of politics more sharply still: for Christians to practice our politics of love on this side of heaven, the only place we have to do so is in the mixed entities of earthly cities. The earthly city is not some kind of optional addition to Christian politics. Our congregations are means of engaging earthly politics, but even they are mixed entities that combine the earthly city and the new Jerusalem. The congregation is not an escape from earthly politics but rather another realm within it, a mixed realm that at least speaks more explicitly of loving interdependence and the reign of God. We cannot practice our politics free of the difficulties, uncertainties, tragedies, and sins of earthly politics. However much we might desire purity in our Christian discipleship and identity, our discipleship is always shaped in *this* world amid its ambiguities. Christians practice our politics of loving interdependence in the earthly city.

17

Christians amid the Nations

In the Augustinian approach we see ourselves as citizens of the new Jerusalem who seek the welfare of the earthly city of which we are part. Our churches are never themselves the entirety of God's work in the world, but they still partake in the in-breaking work of God's Spirit in the earthly city. How then can this approach shape Christian engagement with nation-state politics?

Christians are peculiar citizens in this Augustinian view. While we see state citizenship as secondary or even tertiary to our citizenship in the reign of God, we are not anti-institutionalists per se. As I've said, Christian support of state initiatives tends to be highly conditional. On the one hand, governments make certain claims on us that we follow without dispute. Christians easily abide by just laws that keep order in society and prevent harm, like basic traffic or tort laws. Christians would willingly take many positions in government service as a means of promoting various common goods. New Testament Scriptures speak nondefensively on these matters, such as Jesus saying, "Give therefore to Caesar the things that are Caesar's and to God the things that are God's" (Matt 22:21). In any earthly city, there will be things to protest, but Christians need not protest for protest's sake, as if rebellion is some end in itself. Many twentieth-century Christian martyrs were in fact rather buttoned-up people in their everyday life. Dietrich Bonhoeffer, for example, did not have a reputation as a rebel—seen in his sartorial choices—but he lived out his values steadily and paid the ultimate price.

Yet Christians also hold lightly the claims that nation-states make on us. The state does not tell us who we are, since only God does that. For any earthly city, the temptation to demand an all-subsuming identity will be very great indeed. European nationalisms of the early twentieth century are prominent examples in that they led to two brutal world wars. During those times theologians like Karl Barth and H. Richard Niebuhr said that nations were making themselves into gods, making subsuming claims on human identity. Such nationalism counters Christian politics of loving interdependence, for it desires a state that depends upon itself alone. It demands unyielding allegiance to an earthly city that, Augustine would remind us, is not eternal. While Jesus speaks of rendering to Caesar that which is Caesar's, he also clearly says that which is God's does not belong to Caesar. Similarly, Scriptures speak against the all-consuming claims of the Roman state in books like Revelation, reminding Christians that they belong to the slain lamb, not to Caesar. God's transcendence undercuts any claims to ultimacy that political entities could make. Earthly political power holds no ultimacy; it is not above the law of God.[1] Christians are obligated to challenge state laws when they are unjust.

Because of this ambivalence toward the state, some secular thinkers say that Christians make for unreliable citizens. French philosopher Jean-Jacques Rousseau said as much. Because Christians always hold allegiance to another political entity, Rousseau believed, we cannot be trusted on state matters. But there is also a long tradition of secular political theory that recognizes the potential of states to make overarching claims that harm their own citizens. In this tradition healthy states require checks and balances. The US Constitution attempts to put such structures in place institutionally, but such checks also require strong civil society to challenge the state when necessary. Churches can be an asset here for a state in its pursuit of a just polity, pointing out the flaws that harm its own citizens.

Christians holding their national citizenship lightly also can help navigate times of deep political polarization in a nation-state. In such times, people's identities can get more caught up in their political party affiliation than in the nation itself. With a sense of citizenship based in the city of God, however, Christians need not see party affiliation or nation as their primary political identity. When one's identity in the reign of God takes precedent over party identity, then churches can be places where it's possible to talk across party lines. Someone engages another because they're a Christian who sees the image of God in that person, despite what they perceive as an association with a flawed political agenda. The idea here is not that Christians become helpful to the state in the sense that the state defines the church's political mission, in this case talking across party lines—far from it. Rather, the church's freedom from the state gives it a freedom to seek the welfare of the city or state in ways other organizations cannot, precisely because the church's political identity does not depend on the state. In unexpected ways, Christians relativizing our association with the state can aid the common bonds of a state.[2]

For some Christians, relativizing our earthly citizenship implies that matters like voting carry little consequence. I've heard pastors say "I don't care who you vote for" or "our votes don't matter to the kingdom of God." Sometimes this may be true, yet this approach is also dangerous. Voting kept apartheid alive in South Africa. Voting supported Jim Crow laws in the American South as White people voted to suppress Black Americans. Once again, we cannot cleanly separate God's work in this world and remove it from matters of the earthly city. Apartheid and Jim Crow blocked God's kingdom—they quenched the Holy Spirit's work (1 Thess 5:19). Voting cannot be irrelevant to God's work in the world, even if churches are wise to keep political parties at arm's length. I vote knowing that if my candidate wins, she will surely sin during her tenure, as would I if I were in her shoes. I also vote knowing that sometimes I will vote wrongly. But I vote hoping that it will increase love and justice in this world even in limited ways. We rarely vote with a clear conscience, which is part and parcel of the struggle of human politics in the earthly city.

In short, Christians can promote loving interdependence in our states as well as our churches. We seek states that care for all citizens and that recognize the interconnection of human life. We seek just structures that do not exploit some for others' gain. This certainly does not mean that Christians seek a theocracy—theocracy claims too much divine knowledge for humans. We are too limited to fully understand God's purposes in this world, politically or otherwise. It simply means that we seek the welfare of our city, doing so from the standpoint of Christian love.

An Augustinian temperament exhibits both love and hesitation regarding the earthly city. It recognizes that the earthly city makes genuine claims upon us that we as Christians can see as rightful claims, but its claims upon us are never total. Christians should be strange sorts of citizens in their nations: reliably supportive when it comes to laws that promote love and justice and consistently aggravating when it comes to unjust laws, especially laws that harm vulnerable people. Christians hold our patriotism lightly because our primary political association lies with the kingdom of God. Christians recognize that we are interdependent with the earthly city while also recognizing its conditional quality.

18

The Firstfruits of Public Life

Vibrant local politics enables vibrant nation-state politics. Most nationwide political efforts for love and justice began as something local or brought together many localized initiatives into a nationwide movement. Such initiatives show us that local churches serving our neighbors lead to efforts picked up by wider society. This is true for major policy initiatives like social services and for justice movements like the civil rights movement. Local churches become incubators for the firstfruits (Jas 1:18) of public life.

Since nation-states run many service provisions today, it is easy to forget how many of these programs began in churches. In much of Africa, the United States, and other parts of the world, what is now universal public education drew in large part from earlier efforts by local churches. Churches saw needs around them for education and responded in various ways. Some began on a small scale by offering Sunday school with instruction in literacy. Many set up freestanding schools. As efforts to educate larger populations grew, and as schooling became more important to the labor systems of industrial and postindustrial economies, churches and governments frequently worked together to achieve universal public education. Public schooling is now an assumed part of life in the United States, but it is important to remember that these efforts began locally and often by churches responding to local hardships.

Other features of modern life like hospitals and social services have a similar story. Especially during industrialization, local churches offered support systems when people faced poverty and disease in growing cities. Many hospitals began as ministries of churches or denominations and only later spun off into their own entities. When I walk into my local hospital, now run by a private health-care group, I find a stained-glass window by the entry commemorating the founders of the hospital. It's easy to miss when walking in, but on closer examination I see that the founder began her work through local churches. The story is similar with many other social services: while churches could offer some basic assistance, more sustained poverty alleviation required partnerships with local and national governments.

Churches have inspired efforts for love and justice that caught on more widely. In the examples above, churches were places where people could be creative with new ideas to serve their neighbors. Some ideas worked better than others, of course, but many experiments provided a model since change often begins locally and then moves outward. Programs that worked especially well would get taken up by a city, then emulated by a state or nation-state.[1] The ultimate result might be national, but many such efforts first entailed local churches serving their neighbors.

Some people lament when governments take over such services from churches, worried that they lose their Christian character. Sometimes there is indeed something to lament, as social services can lose a spiritual quality and become unduly bureaucratic. At the same time, however, in many cases having a government take on a social service means that it becomes more reliable. In my experience of local social services, churches do not have the means to keep many of these initiatives going, since church funding proves less consistent than taxation. Once local governments start running such services, local churches need not step aside, for churches and local governments can cooperate with positive results. Churches have networks that social service bureaucracies do not, and social services have programs that churches do not. In one church I served, our emergency assistance program experienced positive changes when we invited a social worker from the city to join us each week. Many people in need found our church a safer space than the sometimes sterile offices of a social services department, so our church served as a bridge institution linking people to wider services.

Not only have nationwide policies begun in churches, but social movements have too. The civil rights movement is by far the most impressive movement of church politics in twentieth-century America in this regard. Much of the genius of that movement was its ability to organize both locally and nationally. It's easy to forget the local organizing infrastructures that consistently provided platforms for people like Martin Luther King Jr., but the movement would not have garnered such national response without grassroots organizing. While people from across the country came to the South to become freedom riders, many of them secular activists, once they got there the efforts were organized largely in church basements. Without those local congregations putting in hours upon hours of unheralded work, the civil rights movement would not have become what it did. Local Black churches were themselves micro forms of politics, and they were the heart of the movement. Their local church politics changed the course of a nation.

The movement also drew from older strategies against White supremacy that were precursors to the movement's achievements, showing the importance of past local organizing. The two Virginia cities where I've lived most of my life, Richmond and Alexandria, each have their own examples. In the early 1900s, Black citizens organized a boycott against segregated streetcars in Richmond, and in 1939 Black Alexandrians staged a sit-in to protest the city's Whites-only public library. Other such organizing happened elsewhere too; it just hasn't received as much attention as the civil rights movement of the 1950s to 1960s. It's a reminder that even when our efforts have limited success or succeed at first and then face setbacks—like the Richmond streetcar protests that were successful early on but then faced a new Virginia constitution that hardened Jim Crow laws—we do not know what seeds our actions have planted.

The civil rights movement furthermore showed how Christians can organize in a religiously plural environment. The movement was by no means an exclusively Christian movement, but the role of local churches was indispensable. Plenty of activists came from other traditions, like Rabbi Heschel, or from no religious tradition

at all. Part of the civil rights movement's success came from the fact
that its Christian leaders did not feel the need to own the movement
as an exclusively Christian one. They were welcoming to outsiders
such as secular young adults from the Northeast, who said they were
surprised to find themselves in church so much. Since Constan-
tine—or at least the Edict of Thessalonica in 380 when Christianity
became the religion of the Roman Empire—Christians have often
felt the need to own political movements. This sense of ownership
and control has led to defensiveness that inhibits interdependence.
Christian civil rights leaders generally did not fall into this trap. In
a more local example, the Hunger Free Alexandria network from
chapter 4 began in a church meeting room and churches proved
central to launching and sustaining it, but it would not have taken
off without secular nonprofit leaders at the core of the movement.

Finally, during particularly difficult times, when it seems that
little or no progress is being made, local action can sustain hope.
There is a long tradition in Christianity of seeing local Christian
communities as embodiments of a new social order that is to come,
working to bring about that social order in their own communities
even when it seems little changes around them. Amid the persecution
of the early church, for example, it appeared that things were getting
worse for Christians. Yet they still believed a new world was coming.
In the twentieth century, H. Richard Niebuhr saw such communities
as cells of Christian activity preparing for a different world. Their
ordinary activity might go unacknowledged, but it can still "create
the conditions under which a real reconstruction of habits is possible," Niebuhr said.[2] Such Christian cells rebuild habits that enable a
different way of seeing and being in the world—a way of seeing and
being that gives hope amid despair.

Keeping hope alive locally becomes a spiritual practice during
difficult political seasons. Maintaining faithful activity when very
little changes around us—or when things seem to be getting worse
—can seem like absurdity to outsiders. Niebuhr said that such ordinary activity looks like inaction in the face of horrible situations. "If
there is no God, or if God is up in heaven and not in time itself, it

is a very foolish inactivity," he said.[3] Especially when using tactics of nonviolence, work for love and justice can seem fruitless for long seasons. Here our church communities sustain hope through practices anticipating a more just and loving future. Sometimes years of patient endurance will suddenly show signs of fruition. Without local political work, hope could not have been sustained. Local politics can sustain the moral endurance that later brings about seismic shifts in politics.

19

The Wisdom of Neighbors

I've spent most of this book talking about Christian churches. But given its focus on neighborhood politics, it would be incomplete without talking about how those neighbors change our churches. Politics naturally draws us into encounters with people of different faiths or no faith. People who don't call themselves Christians—or follow a very different form of Christianity than ours—can and should reshape our church's witness, since the Holy Spirit works beyond our perceived borders of church. Neighbors can show us more about what God is up to in our world.

Take again the example of getting involved in housing affordability. When my church started engaging this issue more directly as housing prices jumped in our neighborhood, a variety of influences shaped our work. Jesus's teachings were the primary influence because he told us to love our neighbors and care for those in need. We saw neighbors struggling to pay rent, and many of us struggled, too. But our discernment couldn't stop there. Again, the question of what is going on should be central to how churches respond to neighborhood circumstances. To answer that question we needed local information as well as more economic knowledge. We talked with others involved with housing affordability in our city; they connected us to secular policy and data experts who told us about local, national, and international policies that contributed to rising housing prices. They told us about the economics of the shift and what local city councils can do and what they can't do amid this housing crisis. Through these experts we saw more clearly how we could respond. These secular neighbors helped us become a more loving community. We needed these neighbors to adequately respond to Jesus's commandments.

After all, a church is a distinct entity within its surrounding community but never fully distinguishable from it. In fact, a congregation cannot really speak of itself as a community without recognizing that it is part of this wider whole; that is, the community around a church shapes it and is part of that church's identity. The borders are porous between a church and its neighborhood. In a mundane sense, a church and its neighborhood or town unavoidably share all sorts of things. They share history. A church participates in economic habits of the community. The industries of the town shape a church. People moving into and out of the town affect the church's membership. A church has to abide by ordinary laws like zoning restrictions. But in a larger sense, such porous boundaries are simply how culture works. Many factors go into shaping a community—the geography of a place, its economics, migration patterns to and from the town, policy choices local and international, and much more. Churches are part of shaping that culture.

When talking about cultures around our churches shaping us, some Christians get a bit defensive. They worry about the integrity of the Christian message, and so they worry that seemingly outside influences will dilute a church's faithful witness. But if we're already sharing history, economic practices, geography, and so much else with a surrounding community, then they're inevitably shaping us. A church cannot isolate itself for the sake of Christian purity in any thoroughgoing sense. More importantly, a fulsome theology of the Holy Spirit recognizes that God's Spirit is already at work in our community, and congregations should harness that work of the Spirit in their own witness. We should not, in the apostle Paul's words, "quench the Spirit" (1 Thess 5:19). Instead we can open our eyes and ears to what the Holy Spirit is doing outside the church.

The question for a church's discernment then is not whether our Christian tradition is influenced by sources we don't label Christian, but *how* it is influenced by them and whether they are shaping us to become more loving and interdependent. Engaging with public life beyond our congregations proves one of the primary arenas in which we engage people of other faiths and of no particular faith.

In politics pluralism meets us head on as we encounter people from different traditions. It is also one of the places where Christians experiment with new practices and ideas that might one day improve and strengthen our Christian witness.

So how do we work together with people of other traditions in public life? One of the most famous approaches to political pluralism aims to form an overlapping consensus between different traditions based on shared values. Even if the roots of those values have different religious and philosophical sources, the expression of values like justice and fairness in public life should be similar enough that people can work together for shared aims. Christians and Muslims, for example, may care about affordable housing for their own reasons —Jesus told me to love my neighbor; Muslims are seeking justice in community. A nonreligious person, meanwhile, might say that they owe certain goods to people in their neighborhood. We can all share the goal of housing people at reasonable costs even if we get there for different reasons. (And in this case, someone can hold all of these views without leaving the affirmations of their tradition; they might just emphasize one more than another.) Other cases involve sharper differences: people of various faiths may all support a truth commission in a town, with Christians, Jews, Muslims, Hindus, and Buddhists having different views on notions of forgiveness and communal justice.[1] They can still share a sufficient commitment to facing wrongs of the past and finding healing in the present. An overlapping consensus between traditions allows people to work together for shared moral aims in public life.[2]

While an overlapping consensus can bring people with differing views together, there will still be disagreements. And frankly, sometimes achieving sufficient agreement is harder within a tradition than it is when engaging outsiders. Some in my own church might wonder why people in the congregation are getting involved in affordable housing or advocating for rapid-transit services. Meanwhile as the pastor, I could be working with a rabbi nearby with whom I agree completely about housing and transit. The greater conflict here is in my congregation as we try to agree on our values as we engage the wider community. Or people of different traditions might disagree about what a housing proposal entails—which communities are prioritized, how housing subsidies are distributed, and so forth. While an overlapping consensus is a starting point, we still need to do community building.

When interacting with neighbors of different religious traditions, or no religious tradition, influence does not simply move outward from our religious tradition to our neighborhood or the public square. Rather, our engagement in public life can reshape our own religious community as well. Some interpret an overlapping consensus to mean that we are all drawing from highly stable traditions as we work together in public. By that reading, influence moves in only one direction as we go from our respective traditions toward shared values and aims in public life. But movement can go in the other direction too because engagement in public life can in turn change our religious traditions.

Aspects of other traditions that we find compelling can and should improve our Christian tradition. As a very practical example, breathing practices I learned from Buddhism helped me weather difficult times when I sat in meetings that were becoming hostile and volatile in congregational ministry or local politics. The practices enabled me to love my neighbor amid bitterness—whether theirs, mine, or both. On a larger scale, when Martin Luther King Jr. encountered Gandhi's nonviolence, it became central to his theology and his practice. Gandhi's ideas and practices, which drew from Hinduism, were not an addendum to King's Christian social action but became essential to it. Jesus told King to love his neighbors, and Gandhi gave him some very practical tactics for how to do so in public life.

The process of incorporating from other traditions is not tidy and it usually involves some synthesis and experimentation, which can be unsettling for communities. Church leaders should know going into such public engagements that conflict will probably come up and they should prepare themselves and their community. Knowing that conflict will likely occur means pastors and lay leaders can prepare for it by building strong constituencies of support amid conflict, by preparing avenues for dialogue amid disagreements, and by showing the community how syntheses and experimentations like this have happened before. After all, much Christian political action that we admire today began as experimentation. To return to Martin Luther King Jr., his "I Have a Dream" speech did not simply draw from Christian tradition. He certainly invoked biblical prophets saying "one day every valley shall be exalted, every hill and mountain shall be made low" and ended his speech drawing from spirituals, "Free at last! Free at last! Thank God Almighty, we are free at last!" Yet he also drew from Gandhi's nonviolence: "Again and again we must rise to the majestic heights of meeting physical force with soul force."[3] He took from the tradition of American democracy, saying segregation spoiled the nation's ideals of life, liberty, and happiness founded in Enlightenment philosophy. We look back on that speech with admiration, for today it seems a natural moment of Christian political action, forgetting that such experimentation with traditions not associated with Christianity stirred controversy at the time.

To hear the Holy Spirit today, we should open ourselves to the wisdom of neighbors. We need their insight to see the fullness of God's work in the world. As much as anything else, politics invariably draws us into life with neighbors. Here too politics can be a means of Christian discipleship, a place where we discover new arenas of God's work in the world in places we might not otherwise expect.

Questions for Reflection and Discussion for Part 4

- How compelling do you find Jeremiah's and Augustine's paradigms to "seek the welfare of the city"? How could it apply to your situation?
- If your congregation closed suddenly, what would the neighborhood miss about your presence?
- What forms of unhealthy hyperlocal politics are tempting for you and your congregation?
- What wisdom are you learning from your neighbors?

Recommended Reading for Part 4

Curry, Michael, and Sara Grace. *Love Is the Way: Holding On to Hope in Troubling Times.* New York: Avery, 2020.

Mathewes, Charles. *The Republic of Grace: Augustinian Thoughts for Dark Times.* Grand Rapids: Eerdmans, 2010.

St. Basil the Great. *On Social Justice.* Translated by C. Paul Schroeder. Crestwood, NY: St. Vladimir's, 2009.

Tanner, Kathryn. *The Politics of God: Christian Theologies and Social Justice.* Philadelphia: Fortress, 1992.

Conclusion

The Body of Christ and the New Jerusalem

J esus Christ has a body and heaven is a city. These two images appear across the New Testament and prove central to Christian spiritual life. We all constitute parts of Christ's body across time and geography, and in Christ we are connected one to another. Heaven is our ultimate destination. Heaven is not a place of individualized bliss but a community pulsating with the love of God.

Jesus Christ has a body and heaven is a city—these spiritual images also have clear political qualities.

We are the resurrected body of Christ. This New Testament theme appears especially in the theologies of John and Paul. John speaks in terms of us participating in Christ's bodily resurrection and Paul in terms of us being limbs of Christ's very body. We cannot be part of that body alone. It is only with one another that we come to constitute Christ's body. I cannot be a piece of Christ's body without another, and another cannot be a piece of Christ's body without me. Alone I do not constitute Christ's body, but with each other we are the resurrected Christ. When we harm one another, Paul says, we are harming Christ himself (1 Cor 6:15–20). When I gaze upon another, I am gazing upon a part of Jesus. When that person gazes at me, they are gazing upon a part of Jesus. We find ourselves constituting the body of Christ especially when our gazes meet in our mutual recognition.

In New Testament times, "body" carried communal and political associations. Still today we talk about a nation as a "body politic." Paul and Stoic thinkers of his time spoke of communal identity in terms of a body with each part contributing to the wholeness that is the living organism. Paul used the notion of a corporate body that was prevalent in his day, while adapting it to Christian thinking. The body of which we are part is not simply a human phenomenon of persons joining one another for strictly social purposes; rather, the body is both social and spiritual. It is a divine body with human members. In the body of Christ humanity and divinity meet together. When forming our Christian life, not only do we participate in one another's lives but we also participate in the divine life.

Citizenship in the reign of God joins us to saints across time and across the world, a political association far beyond the scope of our nation. The body of Christ across geography and history reminds us how small a piece of God's work we see in our specific place and time. On my own, I see only a tiny piece of God's kingdom, but with these others I glimpse the comprehensiveness of Jesus's body. In Jesus Christ, my twenty-first-century identity as an American connects with Christians across the world today, with medieval Christians, with Greek- and Aramaic-speaking first-century Christians.

Our participation in the body of Christ is active, not passive. We are not mere puppets within God's plan; rather, we participate in shaping it. Jesus's body is being shaped and reshaped in our time. God gives the world its own freedom without having to dictate it, which means that we join with God's ongoing work in this world, giving it form in our own circumstances. The Spirit meets us in our common life as we participate in God's work in the world, showing us ever more of Jesus.

Here again, our churches remain some of the most tangible places in which we participate in Christ's body. In our everyday work of caring for one another and caring for our neighbors, we discover Christ anew through ordinary life, whether through caring for people as they age, running feeding ministries, revamping our church coffee hour, or anything else. We partake of Christ's body in blessed bread and wine. It becomes digested in us, becoming part of us so that we go into the world being the very body of Christ. As our participation in Christ's body is rooted in our congregation's worship, so also our politics can be rooted there.

As parts of Christ's body, we look together to the heavenly city. It is our destination, our aim, and our purpose. The book of Revelation describes this city: "I saw the holy city, the new Jerusalem, coming down out of heaven from God, prepared as a bride adorned for her husband. And I heard a loud voice from the throne saying, 'See, the home of God is among mortals. He will dwell with them; they will be his peoples, and God himself will be with them and be their God; he will wipe every tear from their eyes. Death will be no more; mourning and crying and pain will be no more, for the first things have passed away'" (Rev 21:2–4). In this vision, humans no longer look up toward heaven; rather, the new Jerusalem comes down from heaven to us. Heaven and earth join one another.

God's light, love, and life permeate this city. "I saw no temple in the city, for its temple is the Lord God the Almighty and the Lamb. And the city has no need of sun or moon to shine on it, for the glory of God is its light, and its lamp is the Lamb." The city gates are always open: they "will never be shut by day—and there will be no night there" (Rev 21:22–25). Such images of city gates and walls seems obscure to many of us today, as few modern cities have gates anymore. In ancient times gates closed to secure a city from attack. The city of God, then, has no need of defenses. It is a city of peace, without violence or even threat of violence.

Such a city can feel far off from us today. The idea of heaven and earth joining to form a metropolis of eternal bliss might seem nothing like our current politics. In fact, we know that politics can bring on earth something that looks more like hell than heaven. The church has been around long enough to see such hells. The church has been on the receiving end of such hells, as in its early persecutions. The church has also helped shape such hells through its participation in crusades, imperialism, and much besides. Christians both participated in and fought against the hells of colonialism, slavery, Jim Crow, and much more. But such hells are never the end of the story, nor are they our destination. Even when our politics brings hell on earth, we know that our destination remains the heavenly city.

As Christians we pray for dramatic change amid disappointments and failures. We pray for the reign of God to break into this world; we pray for injustices to be broken and our lives liberated; we pray for human communities marked by the overflowing love of God. Yet when I look around and see such brokenness in our world, I've wondered sometimes why I pray these things. I believe that we pray for big things because it keeps us creative and open to the surprises of God's Spirit. If we pray only for small near-term and specific change —vital as those prayers are too—our spirits may not notice when the Holy Spirit is pressing us toward something unexpected yet utterly aligned with the reign of God. Prayer builds spiritual wholeness amid the brokenness and fragmentation of earthly politics because in prayer we connect ourselves to our ultimate destination of the heavenly Jerusalem. When we are immersed in the life of prayer, we can even sense that prayer and political action are part of a single movement of the Holy Spirit working to heal this world.

Our politics of loving interdependence participates in bringing heaven to earth. Heaven touches earth in this life—not fully and not completely, but heaven and earth do intermingle even here.[1] There are times when our politics, local or otherwise, gives us genuine experiences with the heavenly city. It may be as simple as a joyful church coffee hour after communion when we experience a taste of beloved community. It may be as significant as the dismantling of apartheid. But they are all foretastes of the heavenly city, all forms of Christian politics. When we participate in works of love and justice, the heavenly city joins earth. When we feed the hungry, the heavenly city joins earth. When the world sees a church that embodies divine love and the world feels itself drawn to that love, the heavenly city joins earth. The Spirit empowers us to be agents of heaven joining earth.

We can experience these politics week in and week out in our churches. They are places where we shape Christian virtues of faith, hope, and love amid our ordinary lives. They will not always feel like heaven, but there are moments when we sense the new Jerusalem coming down—here, now, today. Through ordinary political life we can participate in bringing heaven to earth.

Acknowledgments

Since this is a book about church politics, I should first thank the churches that helped me learn them. I owe the most gratitude and appreciation to Saint Paul's Episcopal Church in Alexandria, Virginia. Our ordinary acts of neighbor love are the grounding of this book, as are our conversations during Bible studies, adult education events, parish retreats, and elsewhere. Church of the Holy Family and Chapel of the Cross in Chapel Hill, North Carolina, each nurtured a sense of communal interdependence early in my priestly formation. I'm profoundly grateful to pastors and friends in East Africa who helped shape my ideas about interdependence, especially Haruun Ruun and Gabriel Muse.

Thank you to those who read earlier drafts of this book and provided their insights. Through conversations over many years, and through manuscript comments at a crucial time, Benjamin Campbell shaped this book in countless ways, especially its themes about integrating prayer and political action. Charles Mathewes, Katherine Sonderegger, Luke Bretherton, Melody Knowles, Elizabeth DeGaynor, John Allen Knight, Britni Johnson, Mike Angell, Peter John Hobbs, and Daniel Heischman each offered vital feedback that made writing feel more communal. Doctoral students at Virginia Theological Seminary and their wise reflections on ministry have informed much of this book and provided many examples of faithful politics. Richard Bass offered advice and guidance early on, from titles to contents. Christopher Miller not only helped edit this book but, years earlier, suggested I write it during the first class I taught on political theology. When I said that I didn't know of a book offering a political theology for the congregation, he said, "That's your book!" Thanks, Chris.

I first started drafting this book during the COVID-19 pandemic. The pandemic gave renewed appreciation for my most localized form of interdependence, my family. Thanks to Stephen and Philip for the joys you brought to everyday life amid the struggles of that time. And with more thankfulness than I can express, I dedicate this book to my wife Liz, for whom ordinary politics grounded in love seems like second nature.

Notes

Chapter 1

1. This understanding of politics draws especially from literature in African studies, which recognizes and emphasizes forms of politics existing before and alongside state-based politics. Take for example David Beetham's definition of political as "the sphere of collective decision making, or decision making that is taken on behalf of, and is binding upon, any group, association or collectivity, whatever it happens to be, from the family to the state." David Beetham, "Problems of Democratic Consolidation," in *The Christian Churches and the Democratisation of Africa*, ed. Paul Gifford (New York: Brill, 1995), 61. Feminist studies have similarly emphasized this broader connotation of politics. "Politics" has multiple definitions and associations, including more top-down understandings, of course. This bottom-up understanding, I suggest, carries significant theological potential for congregations. For discussion of various understandings of politics, see Luke Bretherton, *Christ and the Common Life: Political Theology and the Case for Democracy* (Grand Rapids: Eerdmans, 2019).

2. I mean violence as inclusive of behavior beyond brute physical violence. For discussion of varying uses of the term "violence," see Judith Butler, *The Force of Nonviolence: An Ethico-Political Bind* (New York: Verso, 2020).

Chapter 2

1. Benedicta Ward, trans., *The Sayings of the Desert Fathers* (Kalamazoo, MI: Cistercian, 1984), 3.

2. Respectively, James K. A. Smith, *You Are What You Love: The Spiritual Power of Habit* (Grand Rapids: Brazos Press, 2016); Eric Gregory, *Politics and the Order of Love: An Augustinian Ethic of Democratic Citizenship* (Chicago: University of Chicago Press, 2010), 21.

3. Desmond Tutu, *An African Prayer Book* (New York: Doubleday, 1995), xiv.

Chapter 3

1. *The Book of Common Prayer* (New York: Church Publishing, 1979), 356.

2. Oliver O'Donovan highlights the political imagery of the Te Deum in the opening of his *The Desire of the Nations* (New York: Cambridge University Press, 1999). Quotations from the Te Deum are from *The Book of Common Prayer*, 95–96.

Chapter 4

1. James Madison, *Federalist Papers, No. 51*, 1788, https://guides.loc.gov /federalist-papers/text-51-60.

2. Augustine, *Confessions*, trans. Henry Chadwick (New York: Oxford University Press, 1998), 1.1.

Chapter 5

1. Thomas Merton, *New Seeds of Contemplation* (Boston: Shambhala, 2003), 13. I am grateful to Neil Balkcom for reminding me of this passage.

2. Quoted in Peter Begans, "Toward Healing," *Style Weekly*, October 13, 2020, https://www.styleweekly.com/richmond/toward-healing/Content?oid =16616796.

3. Quoted in Michael Paul Williams, "'The Lost Cause Is Dead.' Now Let's Dismantle Its Legacy beyond the Symbols," *Richmond Times-Dispatch*, June 4, 2020, https://richmond.com/news/local/government-politics/williams-the -lost-cause-is-dead-lets-dismantle-its-legacy-beyond-the-symbols/article _c349c993-e32e-5fdd-8fd7-8adc60ac7f88.html.

4. Conversations with Benjamin Campbell especially shaped the last two paragraphs.

Chapter 6

1. For discussion of this point, see Daniel Philpott, *Just and Unjust Peace: An Ethic of Political Reconciliation* (New York: Oxford University Press, 2012), 262–63.

2. Martin Luther King Jr., "'Loving Your Enemies,' Sermon Delivered at Dexter Avenue Baptist Church," November 17, 1957, https://kinginstitute .stanford.edu/king-papers/documents/loving-your-enemies-sermon -delivered-dexter-avenue-baptist-church.

Chapter 7

1. Even here, I think, forgiveness still carries political qualities since it responds to embedded political dynamics of household economies, sexual politics, and so on.

2. Desmond Tutu, *No Future without Forgiveness* (New York: Doubleday, 2000), 28. For subsequent discussion by Tutu, see Desmond Tutu and Mpho Tutu, *The Book of Forgiving: The Fourfold Path for Healing Ourselves and Our World*, ed. Douglas Carlton Abrams (New York: HarperOne, 2014).

3. For elaboration of these stages in the context of Desmond Tutu's life and witness, see Michael Battle, *Desmond Tutu: A Spiritual Biography of South Africa's Confessor* (Louisville: Westminster John Knox, 2021).

Chapter 8

1. For discussion of this matter, see Margaret Urban Walker, *Moral Repair: Reconstructing Moral Relations after Wrongdoing* (New York: Cambridge University Press, 2006), 152.

2. For discussions of forgiveness potentially overlooking struggles of victims, see Martha Minow, *Between Vengeance and Forgiveness: Facing History after Genocide and Mass Violence* (Boston: Beacon, 2009).

3. See Hannah Arendt, *The Human Condition* (Chicago: University of Chicago Press, 1958).

4. For an argument that a perpetrator's contrition is necessary for forgiveness, see Nicholas Wolterstorff, *Justice in Love* (Grand Rapids: Eerdmans, 2015).

5. See, for example, John Milbank, *Theology and Social Theory: Beyond Secular Reason*, 2nd ed. (Malden, MA: Blackwell, 2006), 417.

Chapter 9

1. For examples of such adaptation, see The Anglican Communion Office, *Continuing Indaba: Celebrating a Journey* (2012), https://continuingindaba.files .wordpress.com/2012/05/continuing-indaba-report.pdf.

2. See Bruce W. Tuckman, "Developmental Sequence in Small Groups," *Psychological Bulletin* 63, no. 6 (1965): 384–99. Tuckman's approach also resembles discussions about how larger traditions adapt to new circumstances; see Edward Shils, *Tradition* (Chicago: University of Chicago Press, 2007); and Alasdair MacIntyre, *Whose Justice? Which Rationality?* (Notre Dame: University of Notre Dame Press, 1988).

Chapter 10

1. From the book *Why We Can't Wait*, reprinted in Martin Luther King Jr., *A Testament of Hope: The Essential Writings and Speeches of Martin Luther King, Jr.*, ed. James Melvin Washington (San Francisco: HarperSanFrancisco, 1991), 537. Political theology providing commentary on Martin Luther King Jr. is extensive. A few significant works include James H. Cone, *Martin & Malcolm & America: A Dream or a Nightmare* (Maryknoll, NY: Orbis, 2012); Kelly Brown Douglas, *The Black Christ* (Maryknoll, NY: Orbis, 1994); Vincent W. Lloyd, *Black Natural Law* (New York: Oxford University Press, 2016).

2. Benjamin Campbell, conversation with author, March 10, 2023.

3. Walter E. Fluker, *Ethical Leadership: The Quest for Character, Civility, and Community* (Minneapolis: Fortress, 2009), 8.

Chapter 11

1. Cynthia Greenlee, "The Path to Reparations," *Faith and Leadership*, July 27, 2021, https://faithandleadership.com/path-reparations?utm_source=news letter&utm_medium=email&utm_content=Read%20more&utm_campaign =fl_newsletter.

2. Greenlee, "Path to Reparations."

3. Greenlee, "Path to Reparations."

Chapter 13

1. André Spicer, "No Bosses, No Managers: The Truth behind the 'Flat Hierarchy' Façade," *Guardian*, July 30, 2018, https://www.theguardian.com /commentisfree/2018/jul/30/no-bosses-managers-flat-hierarchy-workplace -tech-hollywood.

2. See Samuel Wells, *Improvisation: The Drama of Christian Ethics* (Grand Rapids: Baker Academic, 2018), 87–102.

3. On persuasion and church leadership, see Stanley Hauerwas, "What Only the Whole Church Can Do," *Faith and Leadership*, December 21, 2009, https://faithandleadership.com/stanley-hauerwas-what-only-the-whole -church-can-do. Despite Augustine being a consistent source of inspiration in this book, on the matter of persuasion his record as a bishop became harmful as he came to support imperial coercion against heresy later in his ministry.

Chapter 14

1. At the fall of apartheid in South Africa, for example, Archbishop Desmond Tutu insisted that Anglican clergy should not become members of the African National Congress, the largest political party that had opposed apartheid. Few would question Tutu's credentials resisting apartheid; he simply knew the challenge of getting too close to partisan politics, of partisan politics distracting from the reign of God.

Chapter 15

1. Joe Pettit, "Blessing Oppression: The Role of White Churches in Housing Apartheid," *Journal of the Society of Christian Ethics* 40, no. 2 (2020): 301–4.

2. Willie Jennings, "The Geography of Whiteness: Theologian Willie Jennings," interviewed by Matthew Vega, *Christian Century* 138, no. 22 (2021): 26.

3. See Gibson Winter, *The Suburban Captivity of the Churches: An Analysis of Protestant Responsibility in the Expanding Metropolis* (Garden City, NY: Doubleday, 1961).

4. One difficulty in this regard is that Richmond and suburban counties are different jurisdictions. While separate from city government, suburban counties still depend upon that city for their economic well-being even though they do not financially contribute to the city through taxation.

5. Kathryn Tanner, *The Politics of God: Christian Theologies and Social Justice* (Minneapolis: Fortress, 1992), 107.

Chapter 16

1. The phrase "during the world" as an interpretation of Augustine is from Charles T. Mathewes, *A Theology of Public Life* (Cambridge: Cambridge University Press, 2008).

Chapter 17

1. See Kwame Bediako, "Christian Witness in the Public Sphere: Some Lessons and Residual Challenges from Recent Political History in Ghana," in *The Changing Face of Christianity: Africa, the West, and the World*, ed. Lamin O. Sanneh and Joel A. Carpenter (New York: Oxford University Press, 2005), 117–32; Kathryn Tanner, *The Politics of God: Christian Theologies and Social Justice* (Minneapolis: Fortress, 1992).

2. A work that exhibits this approach is Michael B. Curry and Sara Grace, *Love Is the Way: Holding On to Hope in Troubling Times* (New York: Avery, 2020).

Chapter 18

1. For more on the idea of religious communities taking creative action to address new moral challenges, see Willis Jenkins, *The Future of Ethics: Sustainability, Social Justice, and Religious Creativity* (Washington, DC: Georgetown University Press, 2013).

2. H. Richard Niebuhr, "The Grace of Doing Nothing," in *War in the Twentieth Century: Sources in Theological Ethics*, ed. Richard Miller (Louisville: Westminster John Knox, 1992), 11.

3. Niebuhr, "The Grace of Doing Nothing," 11.

Chapter 19

1. See, for example, Simon Wiesenthal, *The Sunflower: On the Possibilities and Limits of Forgiveness* (New York: Schocken Books, 1998).

2. John Rawls, *Justice as Fairness: A Restatement*, ed. Erin Kelly (Cambridge, MA: Harvard University Press, 2001).

3. Martin Luther King Jr., "I Have a Dream," in *A Testament of Hope: The Essential Writings and Speeches of Martin Luther King, Jr.*, ed. James Melvin Washington (San Francisco: HarperSanFrancisco, 1991), 218.

Conclusion

1. For more discussion on heaven and earth intermingling in politics, see Lisa Sowle Cahill, *Love Your Enemies: Discipleship, Pacifism, and Just War Theory* (Minneapolis: Fortress, 1994).